Writing Your Life

An Easy-to-Follow Guide to Writing an Autobiography

Mary Borg

Illustrated by Ann Blackstone

Cottonwood Press
Fort Collins, Colorado

Requests for permission should be addressed to:

Cottonwood Press, Inc. —— *800 864-4297*
305 West Magnolia, Suite 398
Fort Collins, CO 80521

ISBN 1-877673-07-2

Printed in the United States of America

Library of Congress Cataloging in Publication Data
Borg, Mary.
Writing your life: an easy-to-follow guide to writing an autobiography / by Mary Borg. — 2nd ed., rev.
1. Autobiography. 2. Creative writing. 3. Memoirs. I. Title
CT25.B67   1992   808.02   92-972137
ISBN 1-877673-07-2

The author would like to thank the following for permission to use copyrighted material:

Excerpt from *Stuart Little*, by E.B. White. Copyright © 1945. Reprinted by permission of Harper & Row, Publishers, Inc.

Excerpt from *Growing Up*, by Russel Baker. Copyright © 1982. Reprinted by permission of Don Congdon Associates, Inc.

Excerpt from *The Best of James Herriot*, by James Herriot. Copyright © 1983. Reprinted by permission of St. Martin's Press, Inc., New York.

Excerpt from *Middle Age Rage and Other Male Indignities*, by Fred Schoenberg. Copyright © 1987. Reprinted by permission of Simon and Schuster.

"Milkmen Lost in the Generation Gap," by Guernsey Le Pelley. Copyright © 1987. Reprinted by permission of Guernsey Le Pelley.

The author would also like to thank the following senior adults for the use of short excerpts from their autobiographies:

Orren Gilbert Scholfield, *Many Cherries, Some Pits*
Myrt Grooms, *The Unraveling*
Viola Smith, *Here Am I*
Charles A. Phillips, *Dryland Diary*
Ivan Klein, *The Autobiography of Ivan Klein*
Lila Pritchard Mefford, *Lila; the Story of My Life to 1989*
Joseph Wilson Mefford, Jr., *My Story, My Song*
Uba Stanley, *Uba Stanley's Sojourn on this Planet Earth*
Robert Vail, *Dew on a Leaf*
Barbara Ann Green, *Journals*
Tom Schelly, *Stories of My Life*
Eldon Risser, *The Years of My Life*
Margaret Collier Thompson Barnes, *My Memoirs from 1908 to 1988.*
Mary Koenig, *My Story*
Peggy Hess, *Bits and Pieces of My Life*
Helene Yurman, *Who Am I?*
Julia L. "Judy" Graham, *My Life*
Marie Giesler, *Sentimental Journey*
Pearl Bodendorfer, *Grandmother's Legacy*
Mark Yurman, *My Biography*

To my mother, my three sisters, my husband and my five sons,
with thanks for their encouragement and love.

Acknowledgements

I am grateful to the many senior adults who have taken my *Writing Your Life* courses over the years, who have shared their lives with me, and who have helped make this book possible.

I am grateful to Susan Malmstadt, former director of senior education at Aims Community College, for her enthusiastic endorsement of the idea for this book.

I am grateful to my editor, Cheryl Miller Thurston, for her patience, good cheer, invaluable knowledge, hard work and friendship during the writing of this book, for without her, this book would not be.

Mary Borg

Contents

Introduction —
The Story of Writing Your Life

It all started because of Ethel. Ethel was one of my students in a class called "Twentieth Century American Leaders and How They Changed Our Lives." As the senior adults in the class were remembering the past one day, Ethel got a sad, wistful look on her face. "How I wish I had written down or tape-recorded my father's stories," she said.

Heads nodded around the table. Everyone knew what she meant. They all wished they had done the same thing. Soon they were talking about their own stories. Shouldn't they be writing them down for their own children and grandchildren?

Before I knew it, I had volunteered to teach a class. I agreed to help the group members remember and write about their lives; they agreed to do the work. Everyone got excited, everyone except one cheery, rosy-cheeked woman named Nettie, who said, "Oh, I could never do that. I worked for the telephone company for thirty-four years, and nothing exciting ever happened to me. I wouldn't have anything to write." Still, she wanted to try.

I decided the first assignment should be about ancestors. I made up a list of questions for students to answer, just to get them started, and sent them off to write. Then, with apprehension, I met the group the next week. Had the assignment been too lengthy, too vague, too hard? What if all that initial enthusiasm had waned? What if no one had written a word?

Very shyly, Nettie, the telephone operator, volunteered to read what she had written. Her story included an entire history of the eastern migration of western Europeans to Russia during the latter half of the eighteenth century. She wrote about the opportunities offered by the Russian Czarina, Catherine the Great, who gave free land to settlers. She wrote about the Russian military draft at the turn of the century, immigration to the United States, and the settling of the West under the U.S. Homestead Act. It was a beautifully written story, and she had not referred to any history book. She had simply written what she had learned from listening to her mother's stories. And she had thought she wouldn't have anything to write!

Martha, a woman with no formal education past the eighth grade, offered to read next. She read about her mother, whose husband had died and left her with four small children to raise alone. As Martha read, I could see her mother, a strong pioneer woman who showed her children the small joys of life — picnics, good food, sharing with neighbors. Fun and love were precious gifts, and selfishness, pettiness and prejudice had no place in her world. Martha's eyes misted, her voice quavered, and all of us were deeply touched. In our hearts, we hoped that our sons and daughters could some day write with the same love about us, and that we would leave them with such lovely memories.

The students were hooked. Week after week, I came up with questions and activities to guide them. Week after week, they shared their stories.

Lydia wrote about her father, who was lured to the California grape country before World War I, thinking to make big money. Then one day he came home and announced, "We're going back to Colorado. In Colorado you can brush the snow off your shoulders, but in California the rain seeps through your clothes and you never get warm."

Doris wrote about the day, at age twelve, when she ran after her father with the sack lunch he had left on the kitchen table. She ran several blocks, calling his name, and finally caught up to him. He thanked her and said he could have gotten along without it that day, that she needn't have run so far. And then, with tears in her eyes, Doris read the simple words, "He never ate his lunch that day. He had a heart attack and died at age 48."

Ethel wrote about the childhood summer she and her mother and siblings spent in quarantine because of an illness. Gladys wrote about how she and her twelve brothers and sisters were farmed out to relatives and foster homes, after her mother died. Clyde wrote about Halloween pranks like pushing over outhouses, stomping watermelons, and putting a man's new wagon up on top of the school house. Sophie wrote about meeting her husband-to-be, Shorty, on a blind date. Pauline wrote about plowing through Montana winters and about sneaking over to the Indian burial grounds to find bones and relics of the Sioux.

All that was nine years ago. Since that first, hesitant beginning, *Writing Your Life* has grown into a series of three, quarter-length classes. Dozens of men and women have completed autobiographies, had them "published," and given them to relatives — to rave reviews. Dozens of others have never finished a book, but they have written stories, lots of stories. Even in first-draft form, the stories are sure to be cherished by future generations. Dozens of other men and women are still actively writing, sure to finish their autobiographies in the next year or two.

And now, *Writing Your Life* is a book, as well as a class. I have gathered together all of the materials I have used with my students over the years and, with the help of my editor, Cheryl Miller Thurston, put them into one easy-to-use manual. The book is designed to help anyone write an autobiography, whether writing alone or with the support of a class.

I hope you enjoy the book. More important, I hope you enjoy the journey you are about to take — a journey back through the memories of your life. Good luck!

Mary Borg

PART I

WELCOME TO
WRITING YOUR LIFE

"The longer I live the more beautiful life becomes."

Frank Lloyd Wright

Welcome to *Writing Your Life*

Writing an autobiography is a big task. In order to make that task more manageable, *Writing Your Life* is divided into five sections:

- Part I, Welcome to *Writing Your Life*
- Part II, The Early Years
- Part III, The Middle Years
- Part IV, The Later Years
- Part V, Putting It All Together

These sections contain several kinds of material:

- Information. The boxed material throughout *Writing Your Life* is informational material — material for you to read and use as needed.

- Activities. The activities in *Writing Your Life* are designed to help you to remember and to write. Most of the activities include lists of questions to stimulate writing. Some activities — those marked with a star — help you to remember the past, or to look at the past in a new way. These activities help "poke" your memory.

- Selections from student autobiographies. Selections from student autobiographies are included throughout the book. They are taken from the autobiographies of ordinary men and women who have taken *Writing Your Life* classes.

- Writing tips. Writing tips are included throughout Part I, to give you helpful information about writing. The purpose of *Writing Your Life* is not to teach writing, but the writing tips can provide useful information.

- Quotations. Quotations are included throughout the book, for amusement, information, and as food for thought.

Join a Long Line of Autobiography Writers

Since the dawn of consciousness, people have felt compelled to share their lives with future generations. As you write your memories, you join a long line of autobiography writers.

All writers have different motives, of course, but most people write their autobiographies for some combination of the reasons listed below. Perhaps some of these reasons will be your reasons.

1. To set the record straight, or as a kind of catharsis. Some examples:
   - *Blind Ambition: The White House Years*, by John Dean
   - *The Ends of Power*, by H.R. Haldeman
   - *For the Record*, by Donald Regan

2. To instruct, so that others may learn from their lives. Some examples:
   - *The Autobiography of Benjamin Franklin*, by Benjamin Franklin.
   - *Gandhi's Autobiography: The Story of My Experiments with the Truth*, by Mohandas Gandhi
   - *Memories, Dreams, Reflections*, by C.G. Jung

3. To explain how they overcame handicaps and adversity, as a testimony to achievement against all odds. Some examples:
   - *The Story of My Life*, by Helen Keller
   - *Up From Slavery*, by Booker T. Washington
   - *I Know Why the Caged Bird Sings*, by Maya Angelou

4. To act as historians of major events in which they participated. Some examples:
   - *Commentaries on the Gallic Wars*, by Julius Caeser
   - *The Second World War*, by Winston Churchill. (A six-volume history, beginning with *The Gathering Storm* and concluding with *Triumph and Tragedy*)
   - *The Rough Riders*, by Theodore Roosevelt. (An account of Roosevelt's march up San Juan Hill in Cuba in 1898. A reviewer of the time wrote, "A more apt title for *The Rough Riders* would be *Alone in Cuba*.")

5. To see their names in print. Some people write about their lives simply because they want to, perhaps as an ultimate "ego trip," or because they believe others will be interested. Some examples:
   - *The Boz* by Brian Bosworth
   - *I Kid You Not*, by Jack Paar
   - *The Doles — Unlimited Partners*, by Bob and Elizabeth Dole

6. To leave a legacy. Many individuals want to share their lives with their descendants, or to tell future generations about their world. Cicero wrote, "Not to know what happened before one was born is always to be a child." Some examples:
   - *Growing Up*, by Russel Baker. Baker writes that his children will want to know "how it was to be young in the time before jet planes, super-highways, H-bombs, and the global village of television."
   - *Roots*, by Alex Haley. Haley writes down the stories his family has passed down, orally, from one generation to the next. He felt compelled to record the stories, for fear they might be lost.

- *Yeager*, by Chuck Yeager. In telling about his life, Yeager also gives a history of aviation in America.

7. To share personal knowledge about someone famous (and sometimes, perhaps, for pure sensationalism and money). Some examples:
   - *Breaking Points*, by Jack and Jo Ann Hinckley.
   - *On the Outside Looking in,* by Michael Reagan
   - *Mommie Dearest*, by Christina Crawford.

8. To fill up time. Sometimes people write because they need something interesting and productive to do with their time. Some examples:
   - *Memoirs from Beyond the Tomb*, by Francois Rene De Chateaubriand. (Chateaubriand confesses that he worked on his book to keep boredom at bay, while serving as France's ambassador to Germany.)
   - *The Diary of Anne Frank*, by Anne Frank. (Anne wrote because she had time on her hands as her family hid from the Nazis in Amsterdam from 1942 to 1944.)

9. To tell about one memorable experience. Some examples:
   - *They Always Call Us Ladies*, by Jean Harris. (Harris, in prison since 1981 for killing her lover, the Scarsdale Diet doctor, writes about the "foul realities" of life in a correctional facility.)
   - *We*, by Charles A. Lindbergh. (Lindbergh writes about his 1927 solo flight from New York to Paris in the Spirit of St. Louis.)

10. To enjoy reliving the past. Writing about a life can be interesting and fun. Some examples:
    - *Raising Demons*, by Shirley Jackson.
    - *All Creatures Great and Small*, and *All Things Wise and Wonderful*, by James Herriot.

In *The Best of James Herriot*, Herriot tells why he wrote of his experiences:

> I wrote my books because of a compulsion to make some record of a fascinating era in veterinary practice. I wanted to tell people what it was like to be an animal doctor in the days before penicillin and about the things that made me laugh on my daily rounds, working in conditions which now seem primitive. I suppose I started out with the intention of just writing a funny book, but as I progressed I found that I wanted to tell about the sad things too; about the splendid old characters among the animal owners of that time and about the magnificent Yorkshire countryside which at all times was the backdrop of my work.
>
> They say we should not live in the past and I have no reason to do so because I am still a practicing veterinary surgeon, still enjoying life. But to me, my past is a sweet, safe place to be, and through the medium of these stories I shall spend a little time there now and then.

The Rewards of Writing an Autobiography

People who have used *Writing Your Life* report that writing their life stories is an incredibly rewarding experience. Even those who never quite complete the project say that the writing experience has been a highlight of their later years.

Here are just a few of the rewards real men and women have reported:

Satisfaction. There is satisfaction and pride involved in writing a book. Writing an autobiography is not easy, and individuals who finish feel justifiably proud. Again and again, writers tell of feeling an enormous sense of satisfaction upon completing their stories.

The joy of giving. Finishing an autobiography allows writers the joy of giving a truly special, one-of-a-kind gift. The writers are delighted by the positive response they receive from their children, grandchildren and even great-grandchildren.

Most writers give their finished books to relatives as Christmas gifts. But one married couple wrote their stories individually, had them bound together, and gave the finished book to their children at the couple's fiftieth wedding anniversary party.

Whatever the occasion, the gift of a loved one's autobiography is a special gift indeed.

Healing. No matter how old we are — seventeen or seventy-seven — we are all searching for identity, meaning and purpose in our lives. Often, in the process of recording their lives, writers find that old wounds heal, misunderstandings clear up, irritations with others disappear and the pain of a secret hurt fades. Again and again, writers tell of the peace and understanding that comes from writing their memoirs.

One mother wrote of nursing her son through a year of pain after he suffered first degree burns on three-quarters of his seven-year-old body. For the first time, the woman saw the strength it had taken for both her and her son to survive. Another woman wrote about being sexually abused by her brother when she was very young — and about her confused feelings as she continued to love him, even after his death. Through writing the story, she at last felt peace.

One man wrote about looking forward to his retirement years, only to discover he must spend his days caring for a wife with a debilitating disease. Through writing, he shared his anger and frustrations — and received sympathy from other *Writing Your Life* classmates who shared tales of similar experiences. The support of other writers helped him to face the terrible difficulties he must face each day.

Self-discovery. People who write about their lives also learn about themselves. They discover that they are survivors. They discover that they have achieved some measure of success in their lives — whether mentally, socially, physically, emotionally and/or spiritually. They discover that they have led a life that was the only one they could have led. They have accepted their choices. They have discovered themselves.

Through writing, a person often recognizes, "I really was — and I really am."

Keeping Motivated

Although writing an autobiography is a rewarding activity, it is not always easy. It is sometimes hard to stay motivated, to discipline yourself, to keep going.

Many people work best in a group setting, where they are poked and prodded into action, where they feel obligated to come prepared. If you are a person who needs a bit of structure to stay motivated, try one of the following suggestions:

- Organize an informal writing group with a few friends. Meet weekly to share your writing and to give each other support. Take turns providing coffee and goodies, and make your sharing sessions a special time for getting together.

- Ask your local community college or senior citizen center to organize a *Writing Your Life* class. Or start your own group by finding interested people and recruiting a local teacher to help (offering, of course, to pay that teacher). The teacher's edition of *Writing Your Life* includes lesson plans, tips for teaching, classroom activities, suggested class readings — in short, everything a person needs to teach a *Writing Your Life* class.

  A class setting has a number of benefits. It is easier to keep working because you have "assignments" to complete each week for class. It is easier to stay motivated because you have a weekly audience to listen to what you have written. Listening to other people's stories can jog your memory and help you write. And sharing with others in a class is a good way to solve problems you encounter, and to receive support and encouragement.

- Start, and lead, your own *Writing Your Life* class. Put an invitation on the bulletin board of your church, apartment building, newspaper or senior citizen center, noting the time, date and place of the first meeting. You might want to charge a small fee to cover any costs you anticipate, like room rental, advertising or refreshments. Also, you will need to ask each student to get a *Writing Your Life* book.

  You won't really have to teach; just act as a group leader and make the sharing of writing the focus of class.

- Set up a "correspondence course" with a distant brother or sister. Promise each other to write a chapter a week, and then exchange copies through the mail. Before you start, talk about the importance of being accepting and positive. Brother and sisters often remember events in different ways, but that is because they are different people, remembering things from different ages and different perspectives. It is important not to criticize each other's work — just to share.

You know yourself well. If you know you need structure, find it. If you know you work well on your own, carry on. Either way, enjoy yourself.

You Can Do It!

Relatives often give *Writing Your Life* to their parents, grandparents, aunts and uncles as gifts, hoping to encourage them to write down their life stories. Other individuals pick up the book on their own, with the best of intentions. Then, sometimes, doubts begin.

When it comes to writing, many people suffer from a lack of self-confidence. "I don't have anything to write about," they say. "I've never done anything especially interesting or been anywhere exciting." Or "My life has been just a life, nothing special."

They are wrong. Every life is special. Every life is worth writing about.

Are you one of those people reluctant to begin your memoirs? Here are a few things to think about:

• Think of the dramatic changes you have seen in your life. Those changes range from the technological advances in food preparation, transportation and communication to the problems of living in an overpopulated world in the nuclear age. Besides those changes, you have seen changes in family life, changes in the roles of men and women, changes in the attitudes and expectations of our society. You are an expert on the topic of change; you have survived.

If you were to write about nothing but change, you would have more than enough material for a book, a book that would fascinate your descendants.

• Think about what you remember most from autobiographies you have read, or stories you have heard about famous people. Most of us do not remember much about the historical events, public successes or political decisions that make people famous. It is the human stories that we remember most.

For example, do you remember the details of the Berlin Airlift or the Fair Deal of Harry S Truman? Perhaps. But if you are like most people, you remember more clearly the letter Truman wrote to the music critic of the *Washington Post,* a critic who had roasted a singing recital by Truman's daughter. Truman wrote, "You sound like a frustrated old man who never made a success. . . . I never met you, but if I do you'll need a new nose and a supporter below." People remember that story because it is human — a feisty man losing his temper and rushing to the defense of his daughter. That is something we can relate to.

All lives are filled with stories. All men and women have stories to tell — funny, interesting, embarrassing, painful, delightful, sad or whimsical stories about themselves, people they have known and people they have loved.

You may not be able to recall your stories easily, but they are there. *Writing Your Life* is designed to help you remember them.

- Think about having an autobiography your grandmother or grandfather wrote, or your mother or father. If you had one, wouldn't it be one of your most valued possessions?

  Most people would treasure having the memoirs of one of their ancestors, no matter how "ordinary" that ancestor's life had been. Your descendants are sure to feel the same way.

  No matter who you are, you have a lot to tell. You *can* write your autobiography. It will be fun. It will be rewarding. It will bring you so much pleasure.

  You can do it.

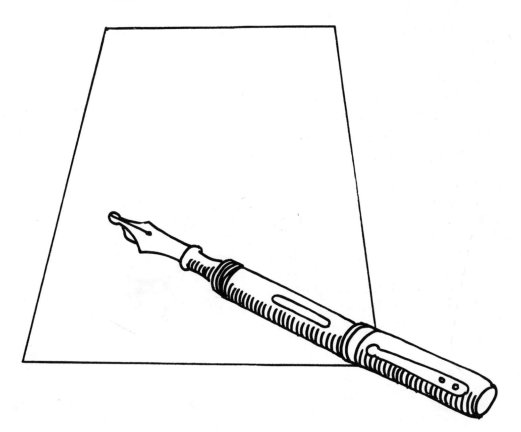

Before You Begin

Make a date with your memories.

Writing your life story will be easier if you make a date with your memories. In other words, set aside a certain time each week for writing. Then discipline yourself to stick to your schedule.

For example, you might decide that every Tuesday morning, from 9:00 to 12:00 a.m., you will write—without fail. Have everything ready before you begin—a certain kind of pen, background music, a cup of coffee, whatever makes you feel most comfortable.

Before the date with yourself each week, let the questions you are working on mull around in your mind. Then, when you sit down to write, you will be surprised at all the work your mind will already have done.

Whatever you do, *don't* wait for inspiration to hit. It probably won't. If you force yourself to sit down and write *something,* you will be surprised at how easy it is to continue. The actual act of writing is the best stimulus for thoughts and ideas.

Be practical.

Use a three-ring notebook for your writing, and type or write on only one side of each page. You will often find yourself wanting to go back and add paragraphs, or even pages, to your work. With a three-ring notebook, it is easy to insert material, and you can also use the backs of the pages you have already written. If you use a spiral notebook, it will be harder to add to your writing and harder to keep your material organized.

Use the questions as memory joggers.

The questions in the activities that follow are meant to be used as memory joggers, as guidelines, as possibilities. Not every question will be appropriate for every person.

In answering the questions, let your writing flow from topic to topic. Don't pause and write, "In answer to question number four, I remember my mother always making us swallow a tablespoon of cod liver oil each morning." Use each set of questions as a memory aid—not as an assignment that must be completed item by item, as if you were back in junior high.

A helpful technique is to take notes as you read a new set of questions. Beside each question, jot down specific incidents or people to write about, as they come to mind. Then you can refer back to your notes as you begin writing.

Believe in yourself.

No one else can write the story you are about to write. Believe in yourself. After all, you are the expert on the topic you will be writing about—your life.

Have fun. You are about to embark upon a fascinating journey.

PART II

THE EARLY YEARS

"Life can only be understood backwards; but must be lived forwards."

Soren Kierkegaard

About Your Family

As you begin writing about your life, don't "get yourself born" yet. Instead, set the scene for your arrival.

Tell what you know about your family and your ancestors. Who were they? Where did they come from? How did they live? The following questions should help you get started:

1. From what country or countries did your ancestors emigrate? Why did they come to America? How? When? Where did they settle?

2. What do you remember most about your mother from your childhood? What was she like? What did you learn from her?

3. What do you remember most about your father from your childhood? What was he like? What did you learn from him?

4. Tell as much as you can about your grandparents. Who were they? What were they like?

5. Every family has its clowns, saints, martyrs, renegades, black sheep, and eccentrics who are deeply loved or loathed. Who were these people in your family? Describe them.

6. What are the oral traditions of your family—the stories handed down from generation to generation? Are there any special stories that are told again and again? Are there any stories known by only a few, stories that are kept secret? (Perhaps there are a few skeletons in your family closet!)

7. What values and beliefs were important to your parents? How do you know they were important?

8. Who came before you in your family? If you had older brothers and sisters, tell about them. When were they born? How much older were they than you?

9. What kind of family did you live in? For example, was it noisy, boisterous, quiet, sedate, strict, friendly, loving, cold, formal, informal? How did your family "personality" affect you?

Writing Tip

A few basics to remember as you get started:

- *Be yourself. Write as you talk, and let your personality shine through.*

- *Don't worry about grammar, spelling or technique; just let your words flow. Later you can proofread and edit—or have someone else do it.*

- *Tell the truth. Good writing is honest writing.*

★ Family Tree

Make a family tree to go with your life story. Be sure to include as much information as possible, including complete names, places of birth, and dates of birth, marriage and death. Leave blanks for information you can't remember or don't know; perhaps you will be able to add it later.

Example:

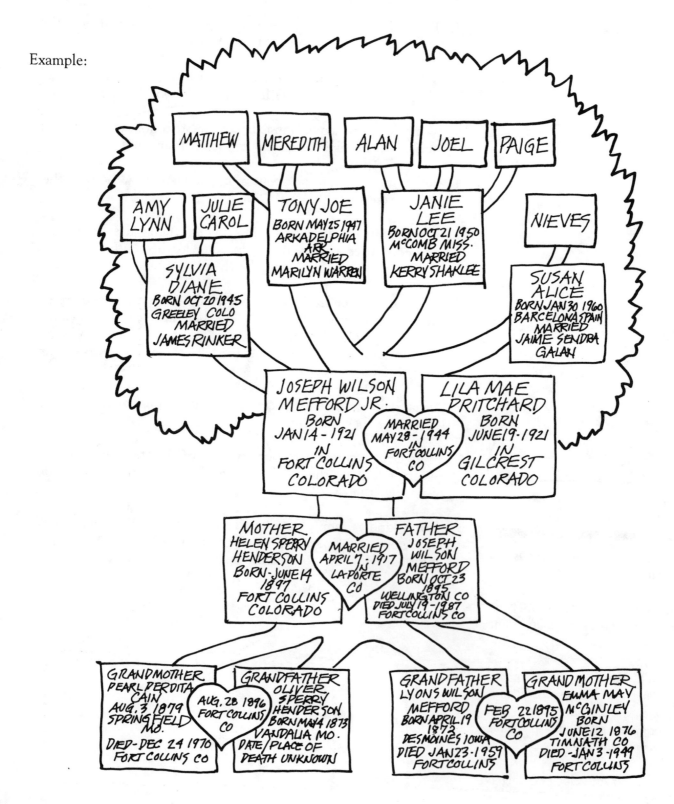

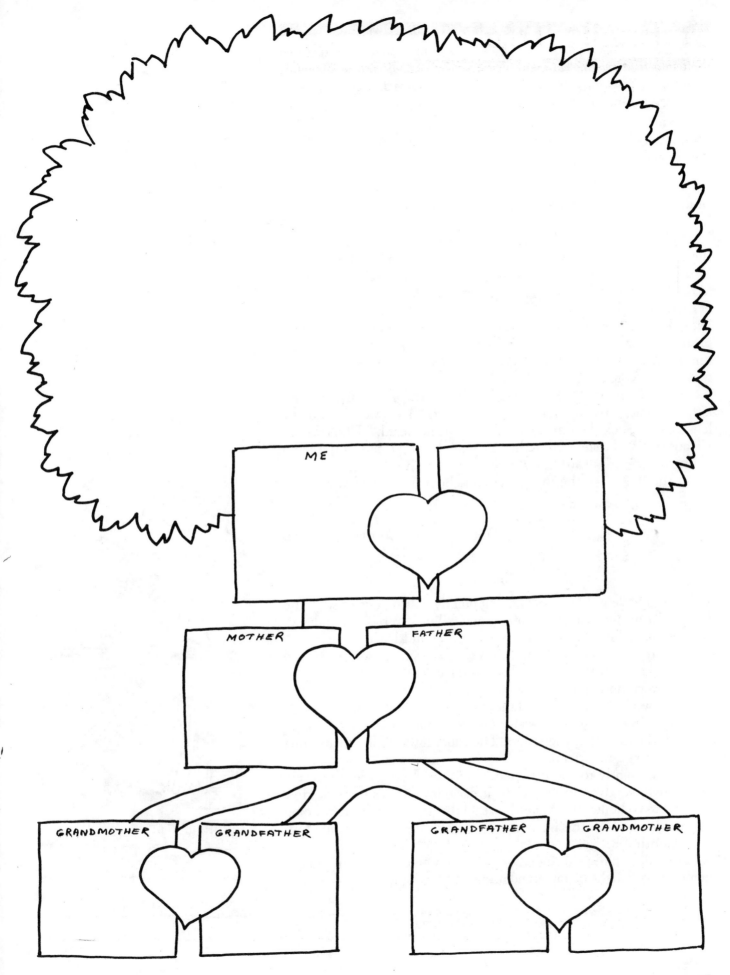

ME

MOTHER   FATHER

GRANDMOTHER   GRANDFATHER   GRANDFATHER   GRANDMOTHER

17

"We all come from the past, and children ought to know what it was that went into their making, to know that life is a braided cord of humanity stretching up from time long gone, and that it cannot be defined by the span of a single journey from diaper to shroud."

Russell Baker, *Growing Up.*

From *Writing Your Life* autobiographies:

My grandfather Leister Scholfield fought in our Civil War with the Michigan Volunteers. In the Battle of Chickamauga he was shot in the chest and left on the battlefield as dead. I have a copy of the letter written by his commanding officer to his father, Samuel, telling of his death. However, he was picked up by the Confederate forces and put in Libby Prison. He was given no medical attention except by fellow prisoners washing his wound with cold water. The bullet that wounded him lodged right next to his heart — too close for doctors of that era to attempt to remove it.

When Grandfather was released from the Army, he returned to his father's home, arriving in the late evening after doors were closed and locked. He knocked on the door. From inside he heard, "Who's there?" He answered, "Leister." His father, Samuel, having received the letter telling of Leister's death, asked from inside the house, "In the spirit? Or in the flesh?" To the joy of the household, Leister answered, "In the flesh."

Orren Gilbert Scholfield, *Many Cherries, Some Pits*

I was a little girl of four, standing quietly, staring out to sea. The deck under my feet was slowly lifting and falling. "Why?" I wondered, "did my mama and papa pack up everything and leave home?"

I was frightened now. Everyone else had the smallpox from having been scratched on the arm by that doctor before we left Sweden. It seemed everyone but me was sick.

They were afraid I would wander off and fall into the ocean, so there was a rope around my waist, tied to a mast. I could no longer climb up the sails after the sailors. The captain was looking after me; he had become my friend.

I clung tightly to the little red box in my deep pocket, my very own tinderbox, given to me by my *farmoor*, my father's mother. How I wanted to go home! But Mama had said this was forever, a new home in a new land, across this big ocean. They said the crossing would take three months.

I would keep the red tinderbox forever. I would treasure it and the memories it bought of my grandmother in Sweden.

Myrt Grooms, *The Unraveling*

18

Finding Out About Ancestors

Many people beginning their autobiographies are surprised by how little they actually know about their ancestors. They become caught up in the genealogical puzzle of hunting for names and dates. More important, they look for information to help flesh out their ancestors and make them real.

If you become interested in your genealogy, there are a number of sources to help you track down ancestors. Most cities have genealogical society chapters, and chapter volunteers will provide you with tips on how to trace family trees. In many cities the chapters also have reserved sections in local libraries.

There are many books, pamphlets and organizations that provide genealogical information. Here are just a few sources that will help you get started:

1. Superintendent of Documents, U.S. Government Printing Office, Washington, D.C. 20402. (202) 783-3228. Three of the pamphlets available (free of charge):

    - Where to Write for Birth and Death Records

    - Where to Write for Marriage Records

    - Where to Write for Divorce Records

2. Family History Center, Church of Jesus Christ of Latterday Saints, 35 N.W. Temple Street, Salt Lake City, Utah 84150. (801) 240-2331.

    These archives are open to the public. They contain census records, courthouse records and information about births, deaths and marriages. When you begin your visit to the Family History Center, you will watch a fifteen minute film and receive a free pamphlet entitled *Where Do I Start?*

    There is a charge to look through the archives yourself, or you can hire a trained, accredited genealogist there to locate material for you.

3. National Genealogical Society, 4527 17th Street North, Arlington, Virginia 22207. (703) 5325-0050.

    Upon written request, this organization will send a list of their special publications. Two of them are *Suggestions for Beginners in Genealogy* (free) and *Instructions for Beginners in Genealogy* ($9.00).

4. The National Archives and Records Service, 8th and Pennsylvania Ave. N.W., Washington, D.C. 20408. (202) 501-5402.

    The National Archives contain federal records on microfilm. including records about the census, military service, pensions, citizenship, homestead deeds and passenger lists. Citizens are granted seventy years of privacy, so documents for people who died before 1920 have just been made available.

    Genealogy Kit pamphlets published by the National Archives should be available at your local post office.

You Make an Entrance

Now you can "get born." Use the questions below to help you recall information about your birth and early childhood:

1. When and where were you born? Do you know anything about your birth? Were you born at home? Was a doctor there?

2. Tell about your name. Do you know anything about your surname and/or its history? Why were you given your first name? Does it have any special meaning? Did you have any nicknames? Did you like or dislike your name or your nicknames?

3. What stories do family members tell about your early years? For example, were you a "good" baby? Did you have temper tantrums? Were you spoiled?

4. Where did you live? What do you remember most about your home or homes? For example, what was your bedroom like? What was your kitchen like? What kind of kitchen tools did your mother use? Did you have a bathroom or an outhouse?

5. Describe yourself as a child. What did you look like? What kind of clothes did you wear? What was your favorite thing to eat? What was your general nature (for example, sunny, shy, serious, quiet, rambunctious, etc.)? Was there a difference between what others said you were like and what you felt like inside?

6. Who came after you in your family? If you had younger brothers and sisters, tell about them. When were they born? How did you feel about their births?

7. Of all your relatives, to whom did you feel closest as a child, and why?

Writing Tip

A few more basics to remember as you write:

- *Include information from all five senses. What did you see, hear, feel, taste, smell?*

- *Keep your sentences and paragraphs short. All of us feel bogged down when we are faced with a half-page sentence or a three-page paragraph.*

- *Avoid "elegant" words. Simple words are more effective. For example, "fire" is a better choice than "conflagration."*

Memory Joggers

Wonderful memory joggers are old pictures, scrapbooks, letters, programs or boxes of "junk." You might be amazed at how memory-provoking they are. Going through old mementos and photos can really help you get your memory juices flowing.

Old papers usually photocopy well, and you should consider including them in your story. Something you think is insignificant or silly might be fascinating to future generations. So go ahead and include a copy of an old report card, a ration book, or a certificate of achievement. Include old deeds, marriage licenses, citizenship papers, confirmation certificates, newspaper articles, school records or any other official papers that might be of interest.

Photographs often photocopy reasonably well and will also add to your story. Include pictures of ancestors, baby pictures, childhood pictures, high school graduation pictures, wedding pictures, pictures of your children. Always identify people in the pictures, including first and last names, approximate dates, where the picture was taken and any other relevant information that might apply.

★ Floor Plan

Draw the floor plan of the house you grew up in. If you moved around a lot, draw the floor plan of the house you remember the most, or of the house you lived in when you were ten or twelve.

Put in rooms, closets, porches, as well as the big pieces of furniture that you recall: the kitchen table, the piano, the sofa, the coal stove, etc. Some of you will also need to draw a path to the little house out back.

As you draw, try to remember the sights, sounds, smells, tastes and feelings from this house. Perhaps you will smell sauerkraut, fresh-baked bread, or your father's pipe tobacco. Perhaps you will hear the squeaky board in the front hall, the old crystal set in the front room, or the slam of the back screen door. Perhaps you will feel the scratchy upholstery on the best overstuffed chair, the swish of beaded curtains, or the heat from the kitchen range as you get too close during your Saturday night bath. Perhaps you will see the back of your mother as she stands at the sink doing dishes, the family sitting down to Sunday dinner, or the jars and jars of peaches, pickles and tomatoes lining the pantry shelves. Perhaps you will taste fresh picked fruit from the garden, your mother's homemade potato soup, or even a forbidden swig of bootleg whiskey.

You are likely to be surprised at the memories your floor plan arouses. Be sure to jot down notes about anything you might want to write about later. Then, as you continue to write about your memories, remember to be aware of the five senses and those feelings, thoughts and emotions they evoke.

Example:

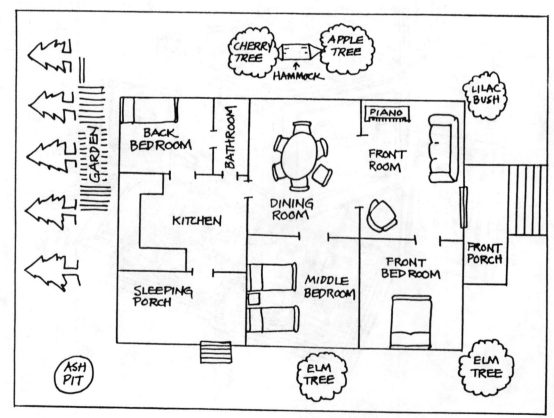

22

Writing on the Dark Side

Fortunately, most memories are pleasant. If we remembered only the unpleasant, our mental institutions would be jammed.

Many adults, however, have memories of historical horrors like the Holocaust, Japanese internment camps or D-Day and the ensuing invasion of the European continent. These historical horrors seem to be easier to write about than personal tragedies—perhaps because they are well-documented and publicly shared by many men and women.

It is much more difficult to write about the personal, private horrors: sexual abuse, the mental illness of a close family member, the death of a child, the alcoholism of a parent, or the unfaithfulness of a spouse. Personal horrors almost always involve other people, and writers are often hesitant to write something that they think is private, something that they think might hurt someone else.

Difficult though it may be, it *is* important to write about the dark side of life. Here are some suggestions that may help you:

1. **Remember that life is not a sugar-coated pill.** You will be doing your descendants an injustice if you ignore the unpleasant side of life. In writing your autobiography, you have an opportunity to share with your children, grandchildren and great grandchildren the wisdom you have gained from surviving hard times, deep personal hurts and/or devastating losses.

   Think of it this way: Imagine that your great grandparents had written about how they fought in the Civil War, survived the trek west or dealt with the high infant mortality rate of the 1800's. Wouldn't that writing be something you would treasure—and probably learn invaluable lessons from as well?

2. **Write from your own perspective.** If you are afraid of hurting others—or of sharing private, privileged information—be careful to write only from your own perspective. In other words, write only about the effects of difficult times on *you*.

   You cannot presume to write about the lives of others or about their feelings. But you *can* write about your own reactions to people and events. More important, you can write about how you survived, what sustained you, what gave you strength and hope.

3. **Writing about the dark side of life can be therapeutic.** Putting words of bile and bitterness on paper can often result in a deeper understanding—understanding of oneself and also of those one may have resented for decades. Often writers will find themselves thinking, "Now after writing this I finally understand. . . ."

   Writing truthfully can help you discover truths—truths about yourself, truths about other relationships.

4. **You don't have to share everything you write.** Go ahead and write about your worst memories. Write your story as if no one else will read it. In other words, be honest. But do remember this: You don't have to include all of these particular paragraphs in your finished book. Whether you include them or not, you will probably be glad you wrote them.

"Everyone is a moon and has a dark side..."

Mark Twain

From a *Writing Your Life* autobiography:

When we got to the pond, my sister Marie sat down and began to take off her shoes and stockings. I begged her not to do it: "You know Dad wouldn't want you to. You'll get muddy splashes on your new dress."

Nothing worked. I got mad and shouted, "Just go ahead. I don't care what happens to you. I wish I hadn't finished your new dress! I'll never do anything for you again!"

Getting no reply, I turned to look back. She was gone. I was scared. I didn't know where she was. I didn't want to go into the water, but she wasn't on the land. Then I saw her head surface.

I was afraid of the water, but everything I'd ever heard about drowning flashed through my head. I hadn't been watching; I didn't know whether this was the first or last time she'd come to the surface. But I had to get her out. To this day, I do not know how I did it, but I dragged her to shore. Then I got sick. When I straightened up, she was being sick, too. I turned her over and held her head so she could spit it out.

Part of me died in that pond. I had nightmares about that day from then on.

This is a story whose lasting mystery was cleared up only after I worked on writing my autobiography. My sister and I have been at loggerheads ever since that day when she was fifteen years old and I saved her life. She always hovered over me, trying to fix this or that, telling me a better way to do something, seeing if I was properly dressed when I went out, etc. I resented that greatly.

She recently called from California where she is in a nursing home near her oldest daughter, and we were talking about writing our autobiographies. She said, "Are you going to tell about the pond story?"

"Well, that's your story," I answered.

"If you hadn't been there, I wouldn't have had any story," she said. "I still don't think I've paid for it. I've always tried to do everything I could, but I still think my life is yours."

"What on earth are you talking about?" I asked.

"You know, the Indian belief: If you save a life, the person saved is responsible for you forever after. I guess I'm more Indian than I look."

And here, for seventy years, I had thought she was just picking on me because she was my older sister!

Viola Smith, *Here Am I*

Being a Child

What was it like to be a child in your early years, from birth until about age twelve? Use the questions below to help you remember:

1. What do you remember with real pleasure from your childhood? Tell about a good time growing up.

2. What was distressing during your childhood years? (For example, did you experience a dust storm, flood or tornado? Was there a family tragedy or death? Did you ever feel abandoned or abused?) Tell about a bad time growing up.

3. Did you ever get into trouble? Tell about a mischievous thing you did as a child.

4. What did you do for fun? What games did you play?

5. What did you want to be when you grew up? Did you have any goals?

6. Did you have a favorite hiding place or secret place? How about an imaginary friend? Describe your "secrets" and how you felt about them.

7. Was anyone ever mean to you? How did you handle that?

8. Was anyone (other than family members) very special to you when you were growing up? Why? How?

Writing Tip

Writing dialogue in your autobiography is usually a very effective technique. Of course you can't recreate the exact words of people in an event that took place sixty years ago. But you can use dialogue to create a general sense of what happened. Because people are always interested in what others have to say, the use of dialogue will make your writing more interesting to read.

Everyday Life as a Child

Everyday life when you were a child was undoubtedly very different from everyday life of a child today. Use the questions below to help you describe your childhood world:

1. Describe your grade school. What was it like?

2. How did you feel about school? Did your family think education was important?

3. What were your favorite subjects in school? What school programs do you remember? Do any of your teachers stand out in your mind?

4. Were you ever quite sick as a child? What was the medical care like? Did your family or neighbors have any folk remedies for illnesses?

5. Did you have to do any chores as a youngster? How did you feel about that?

6. Where did you live—on a farm, in a town, in a city? Describe some of the day-to-day activities common then. If you lived on a farm, you might write about making soap, candles or pickles; milking cows; making cheese and butter; cutting ice; etc. If you lived in a town or city, you might write about neighborhood activities—visiting the green grocer, the butcher or the rag man; playing street games; etc.

7. How did your family take part in the life of your community? Were family members active in church or school affairs? What about clubs, sports, politics or cultural events?

8. What new inventions affected your life when you were a child?

Writing Tip

In writing your autobiography, give yourself permission to move back and forth in time. Your story doesn't have to be entirely chronological.

As you're writing about your childhood, for example, an incident might remind you of a story about your daughter. Go ahead and include your daughter's story out of chronological sequence; it will add interest to your history.

What in the World Is Isinglass?

When writing about your life, remember to explain what you mean. Your grandchildren may be mystified by words and phrases that are common knowledge to your generation.

Take the time to explain terms that might not be familiar to younger readers, terms like *isinglass, clinkers, candling eggs, meatless Tuesday, black bloomers, bobbed* or *marcelled hair, flapper, rationing, charleston, CCC boys* or *McCarthyism.* Also remember that the meanings of words can change over the years. The following words, for example, have very different meanings today than they did fifty years ago: *pot, grass, gay* and *coke.*

The following selection illustrates how little young readers often know of the day-to-day life experienced in the first half of our century:

Milkmen Lost in Generation Gap
By Guernsey Le Pelley

Several days ago I fell into a generation gap. I try not to fall into them more than once a week, but sometimes I run over. I was talking to a 10-year-old friend about my father. In the conversation I said, "His best friend was a milkman."

"A what?" said the youngster.

"A milkman," I answered matter-of-factly.

"What was he? Made out of milk?"

This kid seemed a bit stupid. "No," I said flatly. "He delivered milk. Also butter and eggs. Like the iceman delivered ice!"

The kid's eyes glazed over. "People carried milk and eggs and ice around? For what?"

Evidently this is what happens. Whole pieces of social planking drop out of the structure of history. I can remember milkmen clearly. I can even remember they were the last to give up horses for delivery, because going along a street the horse remembered which house to stop at better than the milkman did.

I could see the youngster really didn't know what I was talking about, so I explained. "People left a note at the door saying how many bottles they wanted."

"Bottles?"

"Yes, bottles. Milk came in bottles. The milkman would pick up the empties, put them in the rack he carried and leave full ones. Then the people would bring them in and take the cream off...."

"Cream? There was a bottle of cream stacked on top of the bottle of milk?"

"No," I said patiently. "The cream was in the milk. The top half of the bottle...."

I could see this was slightly confusing information, so I didn't bother to introduce ragmen to the conversation. Neither did I mention scissor-grinders, who came around fairly often to sharpen our kitchen knives. But I couldn't let him off too easily.

"Later on in the day," I said, giving him something to think about, "the waffleman came by. I could get a crisp, freshly cooked waffle, covered with powdered sugar, for a penny."

When I left, the kid was talking to a friend and pointing in my direction—probably telling him I was from another planet.

And I guess I was.

Remember through Rippling

Have you ever skipped a smooth, flat stone in a clear pond? As it hits the water, the stone makes ripples around the point of impact. Then it skips, and more ripples appear.

You can help generate ripples in your mind whenever you want to remember details about a particular subject. Try this: Write the name of the subject in the center of a page. Focus on that subject and draw "ripples" out from it, jotting down any detail at all that you can remember. Each ripple can then generate ripples of its own. Soon you will have a whole page of memories, and it will be easy to begin writing.

Here is an example of one woman's ripples, as she focused on the subject of her mother:

Example:

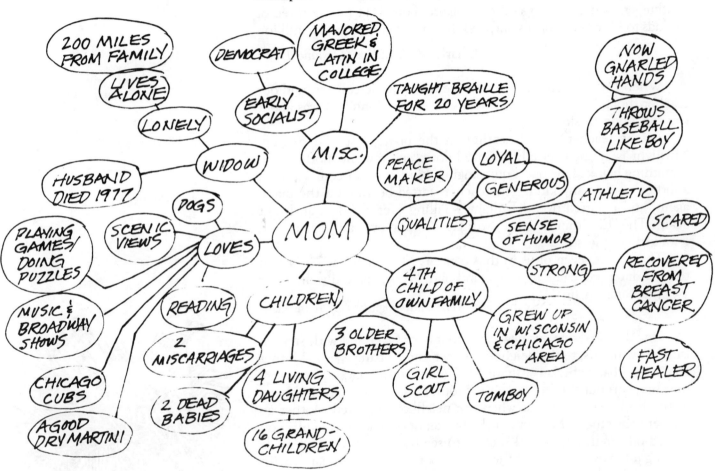

Now do some rippling of your own. Try one of the following topics, or another of your choice:

- your mother
- your father
- school
- brothers
- sisters

"Everyone is the Child of his past."

Edna G. Rostow

From *Writing Your Life* autobiographies:

One fall at school they had a "thing" going about tonsillitis, and the county nurse decided that anyone living as far as we did from a doctor should have their tonsils out, whether they had a history of sore throat or not. They must have been very persuasive because it was decided that three of the Phillips kids should have their tonsils out — my older brother Roy, my older sister Jane, and I.

After the three tonsillectomies, Dad and we three kids walked the fourteen blocks to the train depot, boarded the train, rode the thirty-five miles to the Decker switch, got off the train and walked the half mile home, the only instructions being not to run and start our throats to bleeding. Our aunt Bertha was so mad she could have eaten a goatburger. She told over and over again about Dad taking three of his kids to have their tonsils out, and they never even missed a milkin'.

Charles A. Phillips, *Dryland Diary*

When I was in school, one time we had a music contest, and our teacher thought that I should sing a solo in this contest. I was about the third one to sing.

As the teacher started beating on the piano, I started singing, "Twilight is falling over all." I looked down and saw my mother, and something blanked me out. I quit singing. I just couldn't come up with another word of any kind. The teacher started beating on the piano again, and I started over. "Twilight is falling over all," I sang. I quit again. The third time it was, "Twilight is falling over all," again, and I walked off the stage.

There were seven of us in that contest. My coach saw me out in the hall later. He came up to me and said, "Ivan, you did well. After six, you came in first!"

Ivan Klein, *The Autobiography of Ivan Klein*

One day we drove our new car, a four door Overland with snap-in isinglass windows, to the neighbors' to get some setting eggs so Mother could raise baby chickens. It was a pleasant spring day, and we were traveling without the car windows. Mother was ready to go, and I was in the back seat of the car when the neighbor suggested Mother go see her baby chicks. Mother put the bucket of eggs down carefully and started off. Well, naturally, I wanted to see the babies too, so I made a flying jump over the top of the closed door and landed squarely with one foot in the bucket. In exasperation, Mother sent me home, humiliated and on foot.

That was not the first time she had sacrificed her precious eggs to my caprices. I had also been know to go to the hen house and add six plump eggs to my mud pies.

Lila Pritchard Mefford, *Lila; the Story of My Life to 1988*

Special Times

Every childhood includes special times, whether they are holidays, family celebrations or meaningful occasions of a personal nature. Use the questions below to help you remember special times from your childhood:

1. What was the best gift you ever received when you were young? What was the best gift you ever gave?

2. What were some of your family traditions? For example, did your mother always cook a certain meal for Sunday dinner? Did you always cut your own Christmas trees, or carve jack-o-lanterns together on Halloween? Were there certain routines or habits that rarely changed—like Saturday night baths, the doling out of allowances, or the quiet time given to your father at the end of the day? Which of your family traditions do you hope will be continued by future generations?

3. What birthday do you remember best? Why?

4. What were your family vacations like? Where did you go? How did you get there?

5. What did you do on holidays your family celebrated—the Fourth of July, Passover, Halloween, Cinco de Mayo, Thanksgiving, Chinese New Year's, etc.?

6. What Christmas do you remember especially well? Why?

7. Do you remember funerals from your childhood? How did you and your family deal with death?

8. Do you remember any "firsts" from childhood—your first spanking, first communion, first automobile ride, first trip to the movies?

Writing Tip

As you write your memoirs, keep in mind these two words: facts and anecdotes. **Facts** will help your readers understand the basics—how people, places and events shaped your life. Facts are very important, but it is **anecdotes** that will keep your readers interested and entertained.

Think about the amusing, unusual, uncomfortable, triumphant, frightening, poignant, ridiculous and radiant moments of your life. What anecdotes can you write about these moments?

★ Time Line

Only a few people choose to live as hermits. Only a few unfortunate people are forced by society to live isolated in prisons and mental institutions. The rest of us live in twentieth century America and have been shaped by national events. We are each a part of local, national and international history.

Adults can't help but be affected by the historical events of their lives. For example, the Depression of the 1930's had a profound influence upon anyone who lived through it. So did World Wars I and II. We have all been affected by the social changes and upheavals of the past 30 years — civil rights, women's equality, gay liberation, grey power, the sexual revolution, etc.

While all of us are affected by history, each of us is also a history maker, contributing to the history of spouses and children, and probably of neighbors, community and co-workers. Many people even help influence the history of the nation or of the world — for example, suffragettes of the early twentieth century, prohibitionists, soldiers of World War II or civil rights demonstrators of the 1960's.

Making a time line will help you put your life in historical perspective.

Instructions:

In the left-hand column of the time line, list all the milestones of your life, starting with your birth. In the middle column, record the date. In the right-hand column, jot down what was taking place on the national or international scene at that time. (Use your local library for research. You might include information about wars, economics, politics, social upheavals, etc.)

The left-hand column will become a list of the beginnings and endings that make up your life. The right-hand column will become a survey of American and world history.   For the milestones in your life, you might want to include the following:

- going to school for the first time
- graduating from eighth grade
- moving
- entering high school
- graduating from high school
- entering military service
- entering college
- graduating from college
- getting married
- the births and deaths of loved ones
- times of serious illness and/or crisis
- times of personal success and achievement

Example

My Life | Date | World Events

BORN — APRIL 20·1916 — EUROPE AT WAR

START SCHOOL — 1920 — 19TH AMENDMENT IS RATIFIED
AGE 4   HARDING : PRES.

MOVE FROM — 1925 — COOLIDGE : PRES.
WISC TO   SCOPES TRIAL
WILMETTE, IL

ATTEND CUBS — JUNE 1929 — OCT- STOCK MARKET CRASH
BASEBALL GAME

MARRY DWIGHT — JUNE 1939 — WWII BEGINS IN EUROPE

GR

JULIA BORN — SEPT 1941 — DEC. 7 PEARL HARBOR
DEAD AT BIRTH

GR

MARY BORN — JULY 1942 — RATIONING BEGINS
IN ENID OKLA.

G

MOVE TO COFFERVILLE, — 1942 — WWII IN FULL SWING IN EUROPE & PACIFIC
KANSAS

JANE BORN — JAN. 1944 — ALLIED INVASION OF ITALY

DWIGHT IN — SUMMER 1944 — D DAY
PANAMA

MOVE TO PANAMA — 1945 — VICTORY IN EUROPE

ANNIE BORN — 1947 — MARSHALL PLAN

TRAVEL ON — 1984 — REAGAN IS PRES.
ORIENT EXPRESS

TRAVEL TO — 1989 — HURRICANE HUGO
BRITISH   SAN FRANCISCO
ISLES WITH   EARTHQUAKE
ANNIE'S FAMILY

33

Being a Teenager

For most of us, adolescence is an exciting, yet difficult time. What were your teenage years like, those years from age thirteen to eighteen or nineteen—or until you left home? Use the following questions to help you remember:

1. What did you look like as a sixteen-year-old? Describe yourself.

2. How were you like other teenagers? How were you different?

3. Who were your best friends? How did you become friends with each other? Did any friendships last?

4. What most influenced your life or thinking during your teenage years? Why?

5. Did you ever get into serious trouble at school or with your parents? How were you disciplined?

6. What was the most embarrassing thing that happened to you as a teenager? The funniest?

7. What was the loneliest time you experienced?

8. How did you feel about becoming a man or woman? How did you learn the facts of life?

Writing Tip

After you have written four or five chapters, put them aside for a few weeks. Then go back and reread your work. First, you will almost certainly be pleased by what you have written. Second, you will be reminded of incidents, episodes and details that still need to be included.

As you go back and edit your writing, try to read it as though it were written about a complete stranger. Keep in mind the newspaper writer's questions: **Who? What? When? Where? Why? How?** Be sure to answer these questions for your readers.

Everyday Life as a Teenager

Teenagers of your day were different from teenagers of any other time. Use the questions below to help you describe your adolescent world:

1. Describe popular entertainment during your teenage years. What was your music like? What programs did you listen to on the radio? Did you go to the movies? What dances were popular?

2. What were the fashions like? What about the hair styles?

3. Did you have any teenage idols or heroes? Who were they?

4. How did you earn money? Did you worry about money much?

5. What were kids of the opposite sex like to you? Did you go on dates? What did you do? Where did you go? Do you remember any date especially well? Why?

6. What national and/or international events affected you (for example, the World War I war effort, Prohibition, the Depression, dust storms, rationing, etc.)?

Writing Tip

Has your curiosity ever been aroused by a television report—only to discover you aren't going to get any more details? The details, of course, are what make a story interesting.

As you write your memoirs, remember to give your readers plenty of details. Go over what you have written, and add more detail. And then go back over it and add again.

It may be tempting to write something like this: "Because of the Depression, I never went to college." That sentence doesn't tell your readers much. You need to describe the Depression, telling how that international situation affected you personally. Was your father out of work? How did your mother cope with the situation? How did you feel? Were you angry, accepting, disappointed?

Adding details will bring your story to life.

For Further Reflection—
Thoughts on Friendship

According to Robert Louis Stevenson, "A friend is a present you give yourself." No matter what our age, friends are very precious. Reflect back upon all of the friendships of your lifetime. Use these questions to help you write:

1. Of all your associates and acquaintances, who have been your closest friends? Tell a bit about each of these special people: When were you friends (childhood, young adulthood, middle age, now)? What did you do together? What kinds of support and/or companionship did you give to each other? Can you relate a favorite story about each friend?

2. What do you value most in a friendship?

3. Have you ever gone on an adventure with a friend? What happened?

4. Have you ever been deeply hurt by a "friend"? How did you handle that?

5. Within your family, who has been your best friend? Explain.

6. If you have attended a high school, college or military reunion, describe your feelings about those events. What was it like to see acquaintances you hadn't seen in years?

Writing Tip

When you are writing, try to avoid the frequent use of cliches, worn out phrases like "nipped in the bud," "wise as an owl," "the old college try," "clear as a bell." Make up fresh, new phrases to describe your experiences.

Examples:

"A rainbow is happy dancing ribbons in the sky." Ethan Borg.

"Music was my refuge. I could crawl into the spaces between the notes and curl my back to loneliness." Maya Angelou, Singin' and Swingin' and Gettin' Merry Like Christmas

Just for Fun

Look over the following just-for-fun questions. Perhaps you will want to answer some of them for your memoirs:

1. What bedtime stories were told to you when you were little? Do you remember any favorite childhood poems, games or songs?

2. Tell more about each of your brothers and sisters. As children, what were they like? What are they like as adults? Relate an interesting story or two about each of them.

3. Did you ever attend a circus, major league baseball game, vaudeville show, revival meeting, Broadway play, carnival or other exciting event when you were young? Describe what you saw and how you felt.

4. As a child, did you ever collect anything? What?

5. What radio shows had an impact on you when you were growing up? Explain.

6. As a child, did you have any favorites — comics, clothes, books, movies, toys, etc.? If so, describe them.

7. Who were your heroes when you were a child? Why?

PART III

THE MIDDLE YEARS

"One faces the future with one's past."

Pearl Buck

Organization

Now it is time for you to make an organizational decision. To this point, you have been writing in a mostly chronological fashion. You have followed the events and feelings you experienced as a child up through young adulthood.

Now events and feelings will become harder to write about chronologically. Why? Because there is a big difference between being 5 years old and being 10 years old, or between being 12 and 17. However, there isn't much difference between being 32 and 37, or 50 and 55.

Rather than writing a yearly record of events, you may now want to use a topical form of organization. With topical organization, you write a chapter on a certain topic, rather than telling about your life chronologically. For example, instead of writing about all that happened to you between ages 20 and 40, you might write about one topic at a time, like "marriage," "family life," "career," etc. Of course, it is also possible to combine both types of organization within a chapter.

As you look over the questions in the exercises that follow, think about what method of organization makes the most sense to you.

★ Map of Life

What places in this country—and perhaps the world—have significance for you? Where have you lived? Where have you traveled? Where do your children and other close relatives live?

Use the maps that follow to mark important places in your world. Include a key that is descriptive and uses different colors, perhaps similar to the key in the example. You will probably want to include the following places on your map:

1. Place of birth, with date.
2. Places you have lived, with dates.
3. Places you have visited. Color in the states or countries you have visited, and include the approximate dates you were there.
4. Places where your children live.
5. Places where your parents, brothers, sisters, grandchildren or close friends live.
6. Other significant places—perhaps places from which your ancestors emigrated.

Example

Key:

● Red—place of birth
 1. Wichita, Kansas, April 3, 1923

/// Blue—places lived
 2. Wichita, Kansas, 1923-1927
 3. Enid, Oklahoma, 1927-1933
 4. Sacramento, California, 1933-1941
 5. Ft. Ord, California, 1941-1945
 6. Denver, Colorado, 1945-present

■ Green—places visited
 7. Washington, 1938
 8. England, 1947
 9. New York, Massachusetts, Pennsylvania, 1959
 10. Hawaii, 1982

◉ Yellow—places children live
 11. Patty; Pocatello, Idaho
 12. John; Bozeman, Montana
 13. Lydia; Pueblo, Colorado

◆ Pink—place mother lives
 14. Rocky Ford, Colorado

★ Orange—places from which ancestors emigrated
 15. Berlin, Germany—maternal grandparents
 16. Ireland—paternal great grandparents

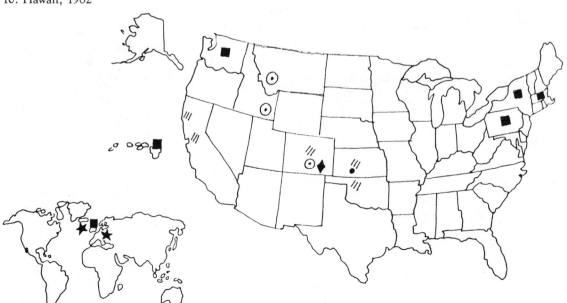

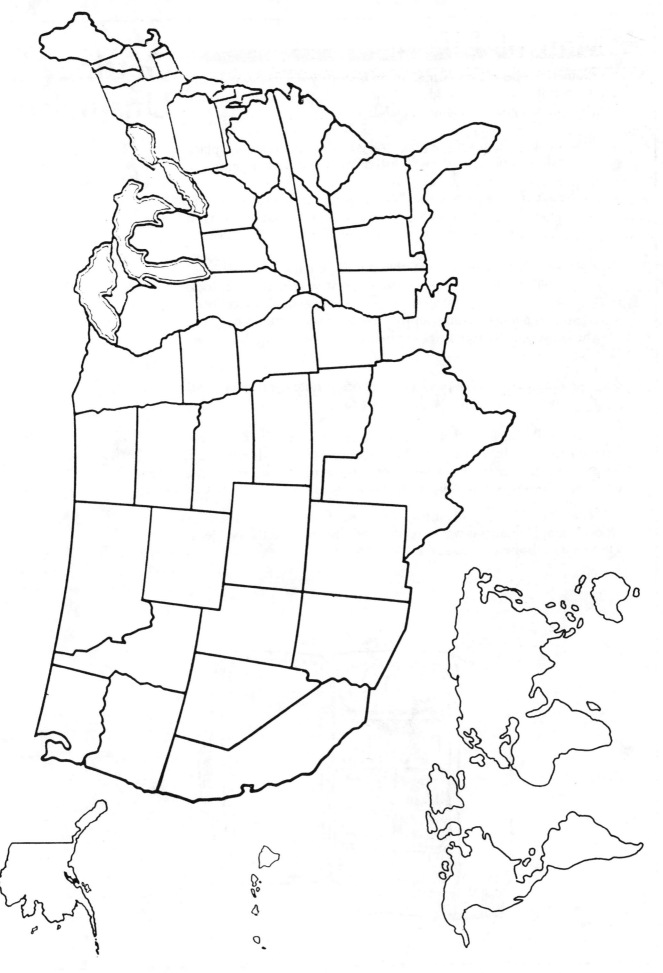

43

Getting Unstuck

Sometimes people get "stuck" in their writing simply because they can't remember certain periods in their lives. If this happens to you, try the following loosening-up exercise:

1. Take the telephone off the hook and go to a quiet room or a place out of doors where no one will disturb you for at least 30 minutes.

2. Now start "taking yourself back" to the period in your life you can't remember. Ask yourself the following questions: What do you look like? What other people are in your life? What are they like?

3. Put yourself in a place from that time, perhaps school, home, downtown or with a group of friends. Using your mind's eye, look at what you see. What do you hear? What do you smell? Taste? Feel? Memories are made using our five senses. If you work on invoking the senses, many memories are likely to come to mind.

4. Take simple notes on a piece of paper or on note cards. Later, use these notes to help you with your writing.

If you still find yourself stuck, don't worry about it. There may be a reason for your difficulty. Instead of becoming frustrated, just jump over the "stuck" period and write about another time. You can always come back—and you probably will, when you are ready.

And remember that all authors sometimes find themselves getting stuck. Ernest Hemingway was once asked how he handled the problem. He replied, "I always defrost the icebox freezer."

Leaving Your Growing-Up Home

All of us—or almost all of us—eventually leave home, ready to become self-sufficient adults. How did you take your leave, thus entering the next fifty or sixty years of being a grown-up? Use the following questions to help you recall information:

1. At what point did you move away from home? Why and where did you go? What did you do?

2. What were your dreams, goals, ambitions as you set off into the world? Did you reject any family values, or even the family itself? Which family values did you adopt?

3. Record some of the difficulties you had in becoming an adult. When did you consider yourself an adult?

4. If you attended college, record a few episodes from those years and their significance in your life.

5. What were some of your early jobs? How did you get the jobs? What kind of training prepared you? Which job was the most satisfying, and why?

6. If you were in the military service, describe those years. What were your duties? How were you qualified to perform those duties? What did your division accomplish? If you fought in a war, what was it like to be in combat, behind the lines? Who were your buddies? What kind of effect did military service have upon you?

7. What was most difficult for you about becoming an adult? Why?

"The hardest thing to learn in life is which bridge to cross and which to burn."

David Russel

Romance, Love and Marriage

There is a reason why romantic love remains such a popular theme in books and movies: it is a subject that is important to all of us. Tell about the romantic side of your life. How have romance, love and marriage affected you over the years? Use the questions below to help you remember:

1. What family stories do you know about love and romance? For example, do you know how your parents or grandparents met and married? Are there family stories about lost love, jilted brides, arranged marriages, elopements, unusual courtships or long, happy marriages?

2. Describe your first love. How old were you? Who was the object of your love? How did things work out? Can you relate a humorous incident involving young love?

3. How did you and your spouse meet? How old were you? What were the qualities and characteristics that attracted you to one another? What were some of the things you did together when you were courting? How did you know you were in love?

4. Write a short description of your spouse—a mini-autobiography. Where did your spouse grow up, and in what kind of family? What was his or her life like before meeting you?

5. Describe your wedding—the ceremony, the participants, the clothing, the foods, the honeymoon. What did you wear? Did you follow any family traditions? Were special foods prepared? Was there a chivaree? Did you have a dowry? A hope chest? Where did you go on your honeymoon? Can you relate a favorite story or two about being newlyweds?

6. Describe your adjustment to married life. What was easy? What was difficult? Were there any surprises? What was it like to join another family and have in-laws? How did you and your spouse resolve differences? What did you do when the road toward married bliss got bumpy?

7. Has there been more than one marriage in your life? How do you feel about adjusting to more than one marriage?

8. If you were ever divorced, how did you cope with the changes that resulted?

9. If you never married, how has being single affected your life? Do you have any advice about being single?

"*Marriage is a great institution, but I'm not ready for an institution, yet.*"

Mae West

"To me life has meaning because we love."

Eleanor Roosevelt, *This I Remember*

From *Writing Your Life* autobiographies:

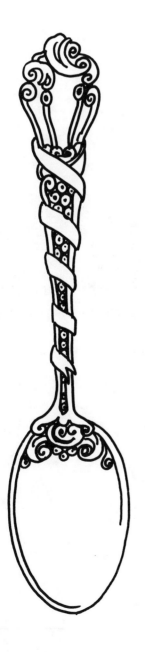

One day my Great Aunt Maude Carlton told me that there were some family spoons, with a fancy "M" engraved on the tip of the handle, which she and Grandma wanted me to have when I married. Of course, this made no great impression on me at the time, and I forgot all about it.

But at my wedding reception, Aunt Maude, now very arthritic and in a wheelchair, pulled me down so she could speak in my ear. "Joe, you remember those spoons with the 'M' on them?" I did remember them, although it was the first time I'd thought of them since I was fourteen. "Yes," I said, expecting her to produce the package right then and there.

But no. Aunt Maude said, "Well, you're in the service now, and sooner or later you'll have to go overseas. And you might not come back. We all hope you do, of course, but you might not. So I've decided to keep them until you come back, if you do come back, and then I'll give them to you. If I were to give them to you now and you didn't come back (There! She'd said it again!), then they'd be in Lila's hands and out of the family, wouldn't they?" I had to admit that was a distinct possibility.

But the bad part of all this is that while I was away in the war, Aunt Maude passed away. She must have taken the spoons with her, for nobody has ever heard what became of them. I just may ask her someday Over There whatever became of them. Most people say that you can't take it with you. But a great planner like Aunt Maude may have discovered some way to do it . . . and she may be willing to give the spoons to us when we all meet over in Heaven. But if Lila goes first and I come after, I'll bet she'll have to wait until I get there for delivery of the goods in question. We certainly wouldn't want to let them get out of the family!

Joseph Wilson Mefford, Jr., *My Story, My Song*

Art and I were married on August 4, 1927, in my parents' home. His father attended the wedding, but his mother did not. She felt her son was marrying below his station. But as the years went by, she mellowed and upon her death left me an electric lawn mower.

Uba Stanley, *Uba Stanley's Sojourn on this Planet Earth*

Children

Before you begin *Being a Parent,* and *Family Life,* be aware that there are many approaches to writing about children. It's a good idea to think about the subject before you begin.

- Some people find it easy to write about their sons and daughters. In fact, they find it so easy that they become bogged down in the details of their children's lives and never really move forward. Be careful that you don't become "stuck" as you write about your children. You have a lot more of your *own* life to write about.

- Many people find it terribly difficult to write about their sons and daughters. They worry about what their children will think, knowing that children can be very powerful "judges," especially when the subject is themselves. Writers may find it difficult to discuss a child who has been a disappointment, who has had an unhappy life, or who has died prematurely. Or they may find it difficult to write because they feel they have failed as a parent. If for whatever reason you find it difficult to write about your children (or a particular child), don't feel that you have to address the subject all at once. Try writing just a bit, knowing that you can always come back to the subject later. Often you will find that, when the time is right, the words will come. It is important to be honest when writing about your children. However, do be aware of balance. Don't write two pages about one child and only two sentences about another. No matter how old children are, they still want to be special in the eyes of their parents.

- Many people choose not to write a section on each of their children as individuals. Instead, they write about parenthood and family life in general, relating incidents about individual children only as they come up in their life stories. They have the philosophy that their autobiography is the story of *their* life, not their children's lives. If you take this approach, it's a nice idea to pay special attention to the last question in *Family Life:* Describe how much meaning each of your children has added to your life.

- If you have never had children, you may choose to skip right to *Job and Career* (page 52). Or you may, instead, want to write about the children who have been important in your life, perhaps nieces and nephews, stepchildren, or the children of close friends. How have these children been important to you? How have they affected your life?

    You may also want to write about why you never had children. Was it a conscious choice? Was it impossible for some reason? How do you feel now about not having children?

Being a Parent

Being a parent is one of the most difficult and most important jobs in the world. Tell about the role parenthood has played in your life. Use the questions below to help you get started:

1. Who are your children? List their full names and dates of birth. How far apart were the children? How did you choose their names? What circumstances were they "born into"?

2. Did you raise your children as you were raised? How are you different as a parent from your own parents? How are you the same?

3. What, to you, is most frightening about parenthood?

4. Did you work outside the home when your children were small? Did your spouse? How did you handle the demands of home, work, children and the community?

5. What have been some of your proudest or most rewarding moments as a parent? What happened? Who was involved?

6. How did you handle the less pleasant parts of raising children—sibling rivalry, bickering, supervising chores, discipline, etc.?

7. How were your children different from each other when they were small? How were they alike? Did you treat them the same or differently? How and why?

8. Assess yourself as a parent. What would you do the same, if you had it to do all over again? What would you do differently? What do you hope your children have learned from you?

9. Describe each of your children. What kind of personality does each have? What have been his or her abilities, talents, disappointments, hurts, achievements, etc.? What makes the child special and unique? Relate some favorite stories about each of your children.

"How many of you know what's important?"

Up went all the hands.

"Very good," said Stuart, cocking one leg across the other and shoving his hands in the pockets of his jacket. "Henry Rackmeyer, you tell us what is important."

"A shaft of sunlight at the end of a dark afternoon, a note of music, and the way the back of a baby's neck smells if its mother keeps it tidy," answered Henry.

"Correct," said Stuart. "Those are the important things...."

E.B. White, *Stuart Little*

Family Life

Family life is one of the strong "glues" of our society, yet every family is different from every other family. What kind of family life did you create with your spouse and children? Use the following questions to help you remember:

1. Did either you or your spouse have strong views about what a family "should" be? Did the views ever conflict with one another?

2. What kind of environment did you and your spouse try to create in your home? Were you successful?

3. What made your family special? Did you have special family words, sayings or jokes? What were your family rules? What were your family traditions? How did you celebrate birthdays, holidays, other special events?

4. What was the most memorable trip your family took together? Why was it memorable?

5. Tell some family stories. Did you ever share an adventure? What humorous episodes can you remember? Can you describe a family hobby, sport or other activity?

6. Were animals a part of your family environment? If so, explain how.

7. What outside events affected your family? Did a tragedy of some kind change the course of all your lives? Did a child's health problems have a dramatic effect on the family? Did luck or fate bring about unforeseen pleasures?

8. Describe how much meaning each of your children has added to your life.

"Home is the place where, when you have to go there, they have to take you in."

Robert Frost

"Babies are necessary to grown-ups. A new baby is like the beginning of all things — wonder, hope, a dream of possibilities."

Eda Le Shan

From *Writing Your Life* autobiographies:

When Cleone showed signs that it was time for the baby to be delivered, we had a problem. They moved her to a cart and wheeled her into the hall, where a nurse said, "Take her back in. The red-haired lady is supposed to be next. The order of patients has already been arranged!" I did not believe what I heard and protested to our nurse, who said, "She is my floor superior; we must wait." Cleone told me, "Honey, the baby IS COMING!" I patted her shoulder and said, "It's okay. Just go ahead and have the baby on the cart, here in the hall. Hold my hand . . . and PUSH!" I spoke LOUDLY so that the nurse could hear what we planned to do, and she went trotting down the hall. Soon the red-haired woman came wheeling back out and Cleone was wheeled in. I was sent to the waiting room.

What they didn't know, and what Cleone didn't know, was that the seat in that waiting room was right in front of an upper air duct. That duct was like an earphone: I could hear EVERY word from the delivery room. Throughout the delivery, I sweated like a furnace room worker, hanging on every groan and sharp-voiced urging of Dr. Sullivan. I knew when Cleone hurt, and I knew why. I heard a play-by-play delivery of the birth of our son, even though I wasn't allowed in the delivery room.

Robert Vail, *Dew on a Leaf*

When our daughters ranged in age from thirteen down to three, my husband decided it was time to take them out West. On the way to a friend's abandoned homestead in the Colorado hills, we stopped in Cheyenne to take in the Frontier Days Rodeo and to outfit the girls with cowboy hats and boots.

From then on three-year-old Cornelia was a cowboy. When I told her that it was bedtime, she said that cowboys didn't go to bed that early. When I urged her to eat her vegetables, she said that cowboys only ate meat.

When we took our first horseback ride into the hills, Cornelia had to ride in front of me in my saddle. It evidently was too close a fit because, although she said not a word, after an hour she took my hand and inserted it between her stomach and the saddlehorn. It was a hot day, and it never occurred to the only real cowboy in the group that we might be getting tired and thirsty. Finally Cornelia twisted around, looked up at me with a sad little face, and said, "Let's go home. I aren't a cowboy."

Barbara Anne Green, *Journals*

Job and Career

Work is an important part of all of our lives, whether that work is in the home or outside of the home. Write about the hours of each week that you have spent at your job or career. Use the following questions to guide you:

1. What jobs or careers have you had during your lifetime? How did you feel about them? Were there certain kinds of work that you particularly enjoyed or particularly disliked? Explain.

2. Would you choose other ways to make a living if you were beginning again? Why or why not?

3. What personal qualities were helpful to you in your work, whether that work was raising a family, being a teacher, tending sick patients, growing wheat, working in a factory, whatever?

4. If you were a homemaker, describe how you felt about your work. What was your favorite household responsibility? Least favorite? Who taught you homemaking jobs? Did you make any wonderfully funny mistakes? What recipes did your family most enjoy? Do you have any tips on running a home and keeping house? What was the hardest part of your job? The easiest? How were your days typically spent once the kids were off to school and the morning household chores completed? (Did you sew, paint, do volunteer work, practice the piano, build furniture, write, read, garden, care for an aging parent?)

5. If you worked outside the home, tell about your work. Jobs and careers vary widely, so use any of the questions below that apply:

    a. What was your attitude toward work?
    b. What gave you the most pride and pleasure in your work?
    c. Describe a typical day. Some of you—ranchers and farmers, for example—might want to describe a typical day during each season of the year.
    d. Describe your work "equipment." What was it like to work in the days before computers?
    e. Describe the pleasures of your work.
    f. Describe your on-the-job worries and responsibilities.
    g. How did you feel about working for someone else?
    h. What was it like to be the boss?
    i. Were you active in the union movement?
    j. Can you tell any amusing, on-the-job stories?
    k. Can you tell about anything dangerous that ever happened to you on the job?
    l. What did you like best about your work? What did you like least?
    m. What surprised you about your work?

"The best part of one's life is the working part, the creative part. Believe me, I love to succeed . . . However, the real spiritual and emotional excitement is in the doing."

Garsin Kanin

From *Writing Your Life* autobiographies:

The colt stopped and nickered. I knew he was getting tired, but we had a way to go, so I urged him on. We had left home early that morning and put miles behind us. My stomach was telling me that it had been hours since breakfast.

We topped the ridge and again paused for a breather. Directly below us was a large valley with several farm buildings. We headed for the nearest one about a quarter mile away. We rode up to the windmill where the stock tank was, and while the horse was quenching his thirst a young man came out of the house. "We're just sitting down to dinner. Would you join us?" he asked. I had lucked out. They were having a late dinner, and I had arrived just in time.

While putting the horse in the barn, unsaddling and feeding him, my nose picked up the odor of fresh-baked biscuits, and needless to say, I was hungry. I hurried to the house and sat down to the table, the young man and his wife and I.

I was surprised to see how meager the meal was, as all they had on the table was baking powder biscuits and corn syrup. But, oh, how good they were!!

The years passed, and I have traveled to many parts of the world. I have eaten in London, Paris, Amsterdam and Vienna. I have eaten lobster in Maine and filet mignon in New York City. But no meal left the memories that one meal did in that long ago time, the meal with that young couple and their baking powder biscuits dinner!

Tom Schelly, *Stories of My Life*

Married women were not allowed to have full-time contracts to teach in Pueblo, Colorado, so I taught various things part-time, like boys' basketball, study hall and a night class for women to exercise. I remember so well looking at obese women lying on the floor doing the bicycle exercise, and I thought, "I'll *never* allow myself to get like *that*."

I'm sure that the Lord lets us live just long enough to do everything we are so sure we will never do.

Uba Stanley, *Uba Stanley's Sojourn on this Planet Earth*

The Middle Years

What was life like for you between your fortieth and sixtieth birthdays? Most of us are busy with family matters, community activities, personal goals and careers. Retirement hasn't entered our heads yet. Tell about your middle years, using the questions below as guidelines:

1. What did you look like as a mature adult in your middle years? How had you changed, as a person, from your younger years?

2. Did life begin at forty? Was it "nifty" being fifty? What about sixty? What personal activities were important to you during the twenty years between 40 and 60?

3. Tell about five significant events in your middle years, either personal or historical. (Remember, World War II is ancient history to your grandchildren!)

4. Tell about the middle years of your marriage. Did your relationship change in any way? Did either of you go through a midlife crisis? Do you have any hints for surviving such a crisis?

5. People often lose their parents in their middle years. How did the death of one or both of your parents affect you? Share your thoughts and feelings.

6. What was it like to have teenaged children? What was it like to have your children move away from home for the first time? How did you feel?

7. Put yourself in history. What was it like to live during the Truman years? The Eisenhower years? The Kennedy years? The Johnson years? the Nixon years? How did the various administrations affect your own life?

"Middle age starts the morning you get up, go to the bathroom, look in the mirror and admit you are who you are going to be. Frightening moment. No more hero, composer, author, athlete or superman. This is it. You are who you are. No more dreams of glory, and no more miracles. Just middle age!"

Fred Shoenberg, *Middle Age Rage and Other Male Indignities*

★ A Few Good Dates

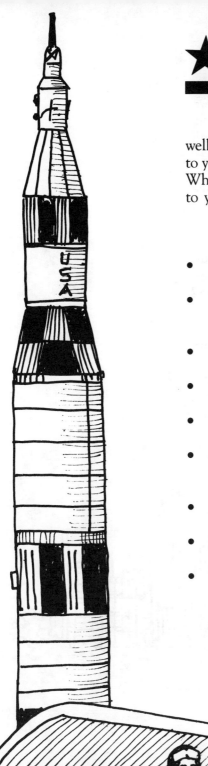

Think of an important date in history, a date that you remember well. Take yourself back in time. Then write about the date's importance to your life and to the life of our nation. Where were you on that date? What were you doing? How did you feel? Sum up the date's significance to you in a paragraph or two.

Here are a few dates that you might try:

- November 11, 1918   — World War I ends.

- May 20-21, 1927   — Charles Lindbergh makes first solo, nonstop, transatlantic flight.

- October 27, 1929   — Stock market crashes.

- December 7, 1941   — Japanese bomb Pearl Harbor.

- April 12, 1945   — Franklin Delano Roosevelt dies.

- August 6, 1945   — U.S. drops atomic bomb on Hiroshima.

- November 22, 1963   — John F. Kennedy is assassinated.

- July 20, 1969   — Neil Armstrong walks on the moon.

- August 9, 1974   — Richard Nixon resigns as President.

Turning Points

In the lives of all of us, there are turning points. Sometimes we are not even aware of them as they occur. Looking back over your life, think about those moments in your life when you took one path and not the other. Use the following questions to help you get started:

1. What were the turning points in your life? Perhaps you had to make a clear decision between two paths. Perhaps outside forces altered your life. Perhaps you forced change into your life because of dissatisfaction, boredom, opportunity or a sense of adventure. How did these turning points affect you and the people around you?

2. What change in your life has brought you the most pleasure? Explain.

3. What change in your life has brought you the most pain? Explain.

4. Do you have any regrets about the "what ifs" of your life: What if you hadn't married so young? What if you hadn't been so strict with your eldest child? What if you had finished college? (etc.)

5. Have your views about what is important in life changed? If so, how?

"When the most important things in our life happen, we quite often do not know, at the moment, what is going on."

C.S. Lewis

"The course of life is unpredictable... no one can write his autobiography in advance."

Abraham Joshua Heschel

From a *Writing Your Life* autobiography:

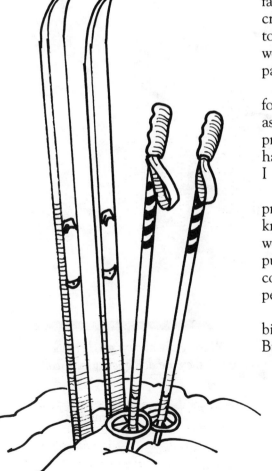

The date was December, 1946. I cannot be more specific, for little did I know that the events of that day would affect my entire life. . . .

A group of us went skiing. It was the first time for me. I had poor equipment, but worse than that, no knowledge of skiing. The company general manager, who was a good skier, had observed my skiing and suggested that I put more weight on the tips of my skis. So, on one of my trips down, my last one, I thought of his suggestion and decided to lean forward a little. I'm not sure what I expected, certainly not what happened. Before I knew it, I was falling head over heels, ending up at the bottom of the slope, still in one piece, but obviously injured. An X-ray confirmed that I had fractured my ankle.

I had been working with Maplecrest Turkey Farms, a firm that produced and marketed turkeys. My work varied with the changing scene — winters in the hatchery, spring and summer in the feed mill, and fall in the processing plant. Now, with my leg in a cast and needing crutches to get around, it was impossible for me to work. I reported to the plant to see if there was something I could do. I was told they would find something for me to do in the office and keep me on the payroll.

I must have left some favorable impressions as to my capabilities, for several months later — when I was back at my former jobs — I was asked if I would like to work in the office again and learn bookkeeping procedures. I jumped at the chance, not knowing what to expect. I had never even entertained the idea of becoming a bookkeeper. But I thought, why not?

Well, that was 1947. For the next forty years, accounting was my profession. I never studied it, but I learned it well in the school of hard knocks. I stayed with the same company for thirty-one years. There were changes of ownership and mergers, but I just rolled with the punches and ended up being controller for the corporation, a holding company with eleven divisions doing more than 100 million dollars per year.

It all started with a fractured ankle — just a hairline fracture, no big deal, no permanent disability. I don't even remember which ankle. But it affected my whole life.

Eldon Risser, *The Years of My Life*

Life's Bonuses—
Hobbies, Travels, Talents

How have you spent your leisure time over the years? What contributions have you made outside work and home—perhaps to church, the community or charities? What hobbies have enriched your life? What talents have you developed? Where have you travelled? Use the questions below to guide you as you write:

1. Is it hard or easy for you to relax? Is it important to you to "play?" How do you spend your leisure time, both now and in the past?

2. Has participating in games been important to you—softball, bowling, bridge, tennis, etc.? Explain.

3. What religious, social, political, cultural or other organizations have you been active in? Describe your involvement in them and their meaning to you.

4. Have you travelled? Where have you gone? What have you seen? What have you gained from the experience?

5. What hobby or hobbies have you enjoyed? How did you get involved? Where has the hobby led you?

6. If you have a talent or special gift, how have you used it during your lifetime? What pleasure has it brought you? What pain?

"People are always good company when they are doing what they really enjoy."

Samuel Butler

Brag Page

It's time to brag on yourself. Tell about the achievements, talents, accomplishments and rewards of your lifetime — and don't be modest. Use the items below to get you started:

1. What public awards have you received in your lifetime? Perhaps you won a spelling bee, a blue ribbon at the county fair, a poetry contest, a top-selling award for your company, a most valuable player award at a high school basketball tournament or a jitterbug contest. Be sure to mention trophies, plaques, certificates, cash prizes or other awards. Include recognition from schools, clubs, careers, churches, charities, communities, hobbies, organizations or other sources.

2. What are your talents, large and small? Perhaps you have been known as a talented singer, a good cook, an interesting conversationalist, a versatile athlete, a gifted artist or a great mom. Perhaps you have a way with animals, an ability to tell jokes, a knack for arranging flowers or an aptitude for leadership. Whatever your talents, tell about them.

3. What special skills help make you unique? Perhaps you can touch your nose with your tongue, recite the alphabet backwards, walk on your hands, play the comb, dance the rhumba or do a great Donald Duck imitation. Have some fun with this one!

4. Tell about the moments in your life that most pleased you, or the times when you were most proud of yourself. Perhaps you saved a dog's life, climbed a mountain, caught a fish, helped a friend in need, lost a lot of weight, conquered a drinking problem, ran a marathon, started your own business, finished a handmade quilt, made a speech or learned to speak another language. What pleased you about what you did, or about what happened?

5. When other people have complimented you throughout your lifetime, what have they most often said? Perhaps they have complimented your smile, your sense of humor, your beautiful eyes, your organizational skills, your athletic ability, your strength, your curly hair, your thoughtfulness or your energy. Tell about your most frequent compliments — and now is not the time to be modest!

"Modesty is a vastly overrated virtue."

John Kenneth Galbraith

For Further Reflection — Religion and Ethics

What are your feelings about religion, faith, ethics, values? Now is the time to become philosophical, digging deeper to explain your feelings about the spiritual and ethical sides of life. Use the following questions to help you get started:

1. If religion has been a part of your life, share your religious philosophy and beliefs with future generations. What do you believe? If religion has not been important, explain why.

2. Have you ever questioned your faith, your god, your church? Explain.

3. Have you explored religions other than the one in which you were raised? What were the results?

4. Did you raise your own children in the same church you grew up in? Why or why not?

5. Do you have a favorite religious story, verse, song or prayer? Explain.

6. Did any clergy member or theologian have an important influence on you? Explain.

7. What does it mean "to be ethical?"

8. What values are most important to you?

"It takes a lot more faith to live this life without faith than with it."

Peter De Vries

Just for Fun

Look over the following just-for-fun questions. Perhaps you will want to answer some of them for your memoirs:

1. If you could be *anyone* — other than yourself — during any time of history, who would you choose to be? Why?

2. Out of all the homes you have lived in, what room have you liked best? Why?

3. *Reader's Digest* used to have a monthly article entitled "The Most Unforgettable Character I Ever Met." Who would be your most unforgettable character — and why?

4. What is your favorite time of year, or season? Why?

5. What is your favorite spot in all the world? Describe it. Why do you like it so much?

6. Have you ever known anyone famous? Who? How did you know the person?

"What a wonderful life I've had! I only wish I'd realized it sooner."

Colette

PART IV

THE LATER YEARS

"One must wait until evening to see how splendid the day has been."

Sophocles

★ Life's Highs and Lows

What have been the high points of your life? The low points? Looking back over your past, draw a graph of your life's highs and lows.

Use the center of a page for "average" times. Then plot high points above that line, and low points below it. Connect the points with a line to complete your graph.

Here is an example of one man's graph:

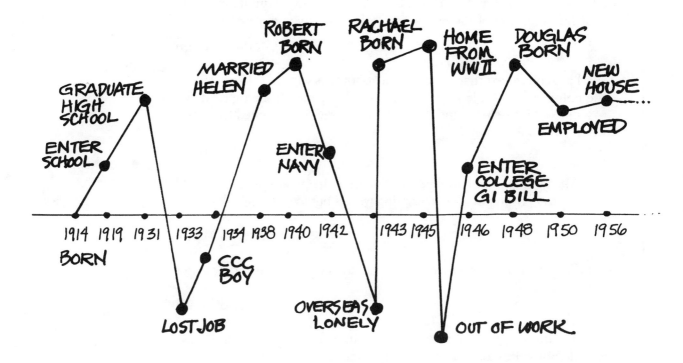

Note: As a matter of diplomacy, it is a good idea to place the births of your children and grandchildren at equal heights.

Now that you have spent many, many hours on your memoirs, you know how it feels to be a writer. It is hard but rewarding work. Perhaps you will appreciate what some well-known, and some not-so-well-known, authors have had to say on the subject of writing:

I love being a writer. What I can't stand is the paperwork.

Peter De Vries

I'll be eighty this month. Age, if nothing else, entitles me to set the record straight before I dissolve. I've given my memoirs far more thought than any of my marriages. You can't divorce a book.

Gloria Swanson

I am convinced that all writers are optimists whether they concede the point or not . . . How otherwise could any human being sit down to a pile of blank sheets and decide to write, say two hundred thousand words on a given theme?

Thomas Costain

All my major works have been written in prison . . . . I would recommend prison not only to aspiring writers but to aspiring politicians, too.

Jawaharlal Nehru

There's nothing to writing. All you do is sit down at a typewriter and open a vein.

Red Smith

Writing is a form of therapy; sometimes I wonder how all those who do not write, compose or paint can manage to escape the madness, the melancholia, the panic fear which is inherent in a human situation.

Graham Greene

If we had to say what writing is, we would define it essentially as an act of courage.

Cynthia Ozick

The man who writes about himself and his own time is the only man who writes about all people and about all time.

George Bernard Shaw

I can't write five words but that I change seven.

Dorothy Parker

The difference between the right word and the nearly right word is the same as that between lightning and the lightning bug.

Mark Twain

★ VIPs

Who are the VIPs in your life? A VIP is a Very Important Person. They are *not* the superstars like parents, children, spouses or best friends. They *are* people who have touched your life in some important way, if only briefly.

A Very Important Person might be a classmate, a politician, a chance acquaintance whose name you never even knew, a pet, a character in a book, a movie star, a buddy in the service, a teacher—anyone who meant something to you in your lifetime, for whatever reason.

List 25-50 of the VIPs in your life, writing a short descriptive phrase about each.

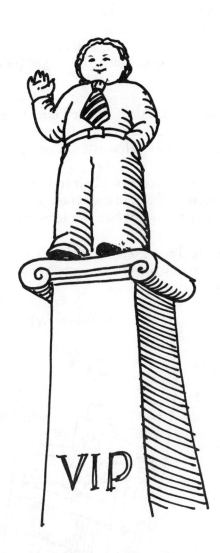

The Later Years

The later years — from about age 60 to your present age — can be a time of both gains and losses. You may have faced retirement and the loss of your old way of life. You may have lost people close to you. But you may also have experienced additions to your life—daughters and sons-in-law, grandchildren, new hobbies, time to travel. Use the following questions to help you write about your later years:

1. How did you feel about retirement and/or the retirement of your spouse? How did you adjust to a different lifestyle?

2. Did you set goals when you retired? If so, what were they?

3. How did you feel about becoming what society calls a "senior citizen"? Mad? Resigned? Surprised? Pleased? Bored? Is it true that "we get too soon old and too late smart?"

4. Have you experienced loss — loss of job, loved ones, good health, sight, hearing, independence, etc.? If so, how have you learned to adjust?

5. Tell how each of your children "turned out" when he or she left home. What difficulties did each encounter? What successes? Where is each child living now? What is each doing?

6. What is it like to be a mother or father-in-law? Tell about your sons and daughters-in-law. When did they enter your family? What have they added to your family? What problems have resulted?

7. What is it like to be a grandparent? Tell about each of your grandchildren. Describe the joys of being a grandparent, as well as any difficulties.

8. What new activities are you involved in? What new thoughts do you find yourself having?

"If I'd known I was gonna live this long, I'd have taken better care of myself."

Eubie Blake

"To me, old age is fifteen years older than I am."

Bernard M. Baruch

From *Writing Your Life* autobiographies:

I am trying to grow old gracefully. I only fight the things I can do something about. I exercise to keep fit and active, and that means keeping my mind active also.

Margaret Collier Thompson Barnes, *My Memoirs from 1908 to 1988*

This is my birth month, and I am experiencing very mixed emotions. I'm glad to have been permitted to live these past 75 years, but I'm dismayed to know that in those years I have lost much of myself.

My mind plays tricks on me, which I refrain from speaking about. My eyes have dimmed, so I now miss much about me. I hesitate to ask what it is that my ears don't quite hear. My balance is more uncertain. I no longer climb up on chairs or ladders to reach things. I now look for the guard rails, and I am more fearful of traffic on the street. My teeth don't fit quite right. I find myself forgoing foods I used to enjoy. The ability to control the body functions is lessened. Embarrassed, I begin to retreat into myself.

Things once so important have lost their importance. Today I might be feeling sad at the loss of those things. Tomorrow I might be defiant, telling myself it doesn't matter that I never became a famous ballet dancer or an opera singer, that I never married a doctor, played a violin or learned to swim or to ride a bicycle.

I used to wonder why folks, as they grow older, get so testy about bathing. Now I know! The unclothed body, once so firm and fit, is now seen as flabby and unseemly. I see in the younger people what I used to have, and in the older people what I have yet to lose. It is harder to get in and out of the bathtub, and it is embarrassing to ask for or to accept help.

As I was sitting at the kitchen table this morning, lost in musings, I became aware that I was sitting and holding my coffee cup in the exact same way my mother used to hold hers. Tears came to my eyes, and I seemed to hear her say, "It's all right, Mary, all is well."

Mary Koenig, *My Story*

I have had lots of joy in my life, and I hope to have more. Hate is out of the picture in my twilight years. Hate never got me anywhere.

Peggy Hess, *Bits and Pieces of My Life*

Across the Generations

You may very well be an important link in your family, a link between five or six generations. Think about it: you knew your grandparents and possibly your great grandparents. You knew your parents. You know your children, grandchildren and possibly great grandchildren. You are in a position to share important observations about your family, across the generations. Use the following questions to help you write:

1. Are there any characteristics or personality traits that run through your family? Perhaps people describe your granddaughter as "smart as a whip, just like her Uncle Dave." Perhaps they describe Aunt Ida as "stubborn as a mule, just like all the Millers." Perhaps, generation after generation, there are relatives who tend to be optimistic, ornery, ambitious, depressed, fun-loving or artistic. Explain what you have observed about family traits over the years.

2. What legacies have you been given from previous generations? What crosses have you been burdened with? How have the legacies and/or crosses affected your life? How might they affect future generations?

3. What was the greatest non-material gift your grandparents gave you? Your parents? What would be the greatest gift your children or grandchildren could give you — or have already given you? What do you hope you have given them?

4. Has any item been passed down from generation to generation in your family — perhaps a shawl, a quilt, a piece of jewelry, a watch fob, a gun? What stories do you know about these items?

5. What life patterns have you seen repeated in your family — for example, early marriage, alcoholism, large families, academic careers, settling in small towns, extensive traveling, unorthodox career choices? Why do you think these patterns persist?

6. Imagine that you could put a message into a time capsule to each of your children and grandchildren, to listen to 25 years from now. What would you say?

"Men in their generations are like the leaves of the trees. The wind blows and one year's leaves are scattered on the ground; but the trees burst into bud and put on fresh ones when the spring comes round."

Homer, *The Illiad*

★ Make a Collage

Some things are hard to explain. How do you describe *marcelled hair* to a modern youngster, or a *buttonhook?* Sometimes it is true that a picture is worth a thousand words.

Consider illustrating the fads and fashions of your youth with a collage. Using old books, catalogues, or other sources, photocopy pictures and drawings of anything "old-fashioned" that applies to your life. Cut up the individual photocopies and arrange all of them on a page, perhaps in a hodge-podge fashion. Label each item, and then photocopy the whole page.

Here are just a few ideas for items you might want to include in your collage:

> fashions—bathing suits, knickers, bobbed hair, etc.
> crystal set
> butter churner
> outhouse
> Model T Ford
> flat iron
> carpet beater
> buttonhook
> one-room school house
> a Palmer penmanship exercise

Changes, Changes

Just by living in this century, you have experienced tremendous changes in the world around you. Take time to look back at these changes and how they have affected you. Use the following questions to guide you:

1. What was life like *without* indoor plumbing, microwaves, dishwashers, computers, television, transcontinental air flight, modern medicine, etc? Write about the many inventions that have changed your life. What inventions have had the greatest impact upon you?

2. What are the most exciting and positive changes you have seen in the world? What are the most alarming and negative changes? Some of the changes you might consider are changes in society, in values and in technology.

3. Do you think attitudes toward men and women have changed over your lifetime? If so, how have these changing attitudes affected you?

4. Because you have lived through so many of them, you are an expert on coping with changes and new ideas. How do you do it?

5. What changes do you anticipate the future will bring? How can young people prepare themselves for the changes they will experience?

6. The role of America in the world has changed drastically in the twentieth century. What are your thoughts about this changed role?

"There is nothing permanent except change."

Heraclitus

From *Writing Your Life* autobiographies:

There was a lightning storm when we lived at 230 North Grant Avenue — in the fall. I was canning peaches at my double kitchen sink. They had been scalded and were ready to peel and put in jars.

The phone rang. It was my brother calling from work to say he'd taken Helen, his wife, to the hospital the night before, and they couldn't tell for sure what was the matter with her. I thought of Helen, remembering how good she'd been to help me during my mother's illness and death.

Something made me wash my hands, take off my apron and go to the hospital.

When I returned home, I found the neighbors in their yards, and one called to me, "Lightning struck close to here!" I looked at our antenna and it had fallen over. I ran in, and the house was full of smoke. I called the fire department. They came and blew the smoke out with fans. They said the insulation in the attic prevented a fire.

I called the insurance man. He came right away and said, "If you'd been at that sink with your hands in water, you would have been killed!" The pipes around the sink were all burst.

Always after that, whenever I knew I should do something good, never did anything stop me!

Peggy Hess, *Bits and Pieces of My Life*

It was pretty bad in the grasshopper days. Grasshoppers would come in clouds and blot out the sun. They were so thick sometimes that you would look at a fence post and you couldn't see the post—just solid grasshoppers. It looked like a post of grasshoppers.

Every morning we would spread grasshopper poison, which was a bran made up of a poison and banana oil. There would be a lot of grasshoppers die from that poison. You would see them thick on the ground, just as thick as could be.

We made a grasshopper catcher about 16 feet wide. It was about three or four feet wide at the bottom, and then it came straight up the back and slanted up. The slanted part was lined with tin. We would put two horses on the catcher and drive it down the hay field.

The grasshoppers would hit the tin, and then they couldn't hang on to it. They would slide down and get into a slot like a fly catcher in the back end. There was a box back there, and when we got to the end of the field we would spray the grasshoppers with a kerosene sprayer. They couldn't fly, and it wouldn't be very long and they would die from the spray.

When we got to the end of the field, we would take a scoop shovel and scoop those grasshoppers out of there and put them in a pile. I mean, there were piles three and four feet high, hundreds and hundreds of pounds of grasshoppers laying on every end of the field. It smelled pretty bad, too, after a few days.

Ivan Klein, *The Autobiography of Ivan Klein*

Secrets

There is an old saying that "What you don't know won't hurt you." However, there is more and more evidence that secrets in a family have long lasting, far-reaching effects, even through future generations. Incest, spouse abuse, child abuse, alcoholism, teenage pregnancy and depression all tend to reappear in families, generation after generation. In fact, some psychologists believe that families who don't acknowledge and deal with their secrets are doomed to repeat them. Families may be able to break destructive patterns only when those patterns are brought out into the open and addressed.

Just as it is important to record medical history for children and grandchildren, it is important to help them understand the truth about the lives of people close to them. For example, it may be important for children to know that their mother suffered abuse from an alcoholic father, or that tensions they remember from early years resulted from a family bankruptcy. People can deal with reality only when they know the truth.

In the telling, family secrets often make profound differences in the lives of children and grandchildren. Understanding can never come too late.

Use the following questions to help you write about secrets in your family:

1. Are there any family secrets you have discovered that you wish you had known about much earlier? Explain.

2. Are there any misconceptions or misunderstandings that have persisted between you and another person over the years? Explain.

3. Are there any mysteries in your life that you wonder about, mysteries which have never been cleared up? Do you think you would be different if you knew the truth?

4. Are there any members of your family from whom you have tried to conceal certain truths? Why? Are there any who have tried to conceal truths from you?

5. Is there anything people believe about you that is incorrect?

6. Are there any secrets you would like to share with your children and grandchildren?

"If you cannot get rid of the family skeleton, you may as well make it dance."

George Bernard Shaw

Likes and Dislikes

Everybody has likes and dislikes. What are yours? Use the following questions to help spark your memory:

1. What are your favorites? List your favorites from any of the categories below, and add any others that appeal to you. If you would like, add a short explanation beside each item.

   - books
   - songs
   - television shows
   - movies
   - plays
   - kinds of music
   - colors
   - foods
   - flowers
   - operas
   - holidays
   - sports
   - cities
   - restaurants
   - dances
   - presidents
   - people's names

2. Look at the categories above. Do items you particularly *dislike* come to mind?

3. What are your pet peeves — those annoying little things that drive you to distraction?

4. What would you still like to learn? What things would you like to learn more about?

"The world is so full of a number of things,
  I'm sure we should all be as happy as kings."

Robert Louis Stevenson

★ The Ten Commandments We Live By

As Americans, most of us have been raised in the Judeo-Christian tradition, which stresses the importance of living by the Ten Commandments. However, it is seldom that we relate these Commandments to our daily lives. Very few of us, after all, have trouble *not* killing, stealing or creating graven images on any given weekday.

No, it's not the Ten Commandments that we really live by. What we really live by are all those adages taught to us as children by our parents and grandparents. These sayings, proverbs and messages about life have an enormous impact on our daily lives. Often we are not aware of how deeply the philosophies have affected us, or of how much they have become our own.

Using the space below, jot down the messages you heard as you were growing up. Here are a few examples other adults have shared:

1. Honest work never hurt anyone.

2. Use it up, wear it out, make it do or do without.

3. Cleanliness is next to godliness.

4. There is only one way to get the milkin' done, and that's to get to milkin'.

5. If you can't afford it, don't buy it.

6. The road to Hell is paved with good intentions.

7. Let your conscience be your guide.

8. Whatever is worth doing is worth doing well.

9. If you can't say something nice, don't say anything at all.

10. Life is what you make of it.

After you complete your list, write about the effects these messages have had upon you. Were the messages valid in your life? Why or why not?

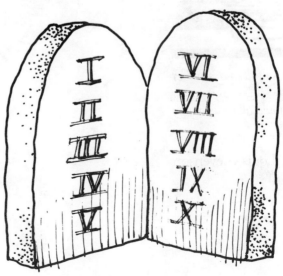

76

Giving Advice

We all love to give advice. Here is your opportunity! What advice do you have for future generations about any of the following topics, or others?

- politics and political parties
- getting along with others
- money — both hard cash and credit
- happiness
- religion
- raising kids
- coping with hard times
- love
- giving
- work
- marriage

"With the ancient is wisdom; and in length of years understanding."

The Old Testament, *Job*

Who Are You — Really?

If you are like most people, the face you show the world may disguise your true self — or tell only part of the story. Tell about who you *really* are — the self inside of you, your hopes, dreams, philosophies, worries, etc. Use the following questions to help you get started:

1. Describe the intellectual you. What do you like to think about, read about, learn about?

2. Describe the spiritual you. What do you care about deeply?

3. Describe the emotional you. For example, are you pessimistic or optimistic by nature? How do you feel and show love, hate, joy, sorrow, satisfaction, anger, etc.?

4. What hopes or dreams have you had during your lifetime? Which ones have come true? Which ones have not? What do you still dream about?

5. Describe your philosophy of life. You probably have one, even if you have never put it into words. What concepts or principles motivate you? What are the values by which you live?

6. What have you had to learn over and over?

7. What one period of your life would you like to relive if you could? Why?

8. If you could choose a symbol for your life, what would you pick? Would it be an animal, a building, a bird, a geometric figure, something else? Why would the symbol describe you?

"At bottom every man knows well enough that he is a unique being, only once on this earth; and by no extraordinary chance will such a marvelously picturesque piece of diversity in unity as he is, ever be put together a second time."

Friedrich Nietzsche

"I should not talk so much about myself if there were somebody else whom I knew as well."

Henry D. Thoreau

From a *Writing Your Life* autobiography:

I used to be 5'5" plus but now have shrunk, as the vertebrae have pulled together, to 5'4." Yet other people see me as taller than I do, possibly because I try to stand straight to avoid a dowager's hump, and to feel taller. There is a trait in my family called the Serge walk (Mother's maiden name was Serge, and she and all her sisters walked this way, as does my own sister): the body angles forward from the hips, and the shoulders hunch forward as the head lurches along. It should be called the tension trot. I try hard to avoid it. Sneaking a furtive look in a store window glass helps.

My hair is almost totally white now. There is a trace of the original black around the nape of my neck. I still remember the white streak that decorated the front of my hair when I was in high school, years before it became fashionable to paint that streak in with chemicals. (How come eyebrows remain black when the rest of the head hair turns all white?) Maybe that explains my preoccupation with the combination of black and white in the wardrobe I prefer. For years I made clothing for myself predominantly in black, white and gray. I even made an afghan in that combination to go with a sofa bed in black-and-white tweed. My car is white with black trim. Am I flaunting my black-and-white flag on top?

Intellectual growth is an ongoing process that seems to accelerate in senior years rather than slow down, in my case anyway. A slow learner? Perhaps I just have more time now to analyze what I am gathering from all the media, books, conversations and experiences. At least I feel I am freer to absorb what comes my way, retain what is essential or appropriate, and discard what I decide is neither of the latter, or what I frivolously feel is ridiculous or obscenely aggravating. When I was younger and a working mother and wife, there were not enough hours left over for much intellectual anything.

My mother advocated equal rights for women in her high school valedictory speech, then married a physician and devoted her life to his needs. My father was a strict disciplinarian with very high standards of behavior. The conflict those two created in me has resulted in a few major battles and many minor skirmishes between my mind and my heart. Friends and associates tell me they see in me a strong person with nonconforming originality. I acknowledge the rebellions but not the strength. I see myself as a follower who has been placed in a lead position reluctantly on occasion. I cry at parades but am depended upon in crises. I give up in the face of authority but press on in the face of stupidity. I am gregarious but treasure those quiet times at home.

Who is so brave as to judge which is the *real* person? The one we think we are or the one the world tells us we are? I feel we present different persons to different groups of people, out of sensitivity or expectations or fears. We could and probably do spend our lifetimes trying to find the answers. That's only part of the fun.

Helene Yurman, *Who Am I?*

For Further Reflection — Looking Back

As we look back upon our lives, we are able to put things into perspective. We see things more clearly. Look back over your life to answer the following questions:

1. Out of the thousands of events in your lifetime — positive or negative — pick five that have shaped your life. Describe them.

2. What was the saddest or most painful time of your life? Why? How did you deal with the pain? Because of that pain, how are you different?

3. What has been the happiest or most joyous time of your life? Explain.

4. What do you feel has been your greatest achievement in life? What are you most proud of? Explain.

5. If you had your life to live over, what *one* thing would you do differently?

"The past is the present, isn't it? It's the future, too. We all tried to lie out of that, but life won't let us."

Eugene O'Neill

Just for Fun

Just for fun, try writing a paragraph or essay on any of the following topics:

- If Only I'd Known Then What I Know Now
- Doctors and Dentists I Have Known
- An Embarrassing Moment
- Pets (or Other Animals) in My Life
- The Best Meal I Ever Ate
- Dreams and Nightmares
- Something I Just Can't Explain

"'How old would you be if you didn't know how old you were?"

Satchel Paige

PART V

PUTTING IT ALL TOGETHER

"I think I did pretty well, considering I started out with nothing but a bunch of blank paper."

Steve Martin

Putting It All Together

You have finished writing your memoirs. Now what? You probably have pages and pages of material, dozens of photos and a collection of documents, letters, certificates and other memorabilia. How do you put it all together so that your relatives — and you — can enjoy it?

Use the information that follows to help you. Soon you will have a finished book, a book that your descendants are sure to treasure for years to come.

Before your book is typed, you will need to take care of some details — editing and proofreading. Editing and proofreading are essential to making your book the very best it can be.

Editing

Editing is the first step in turning your finished material into a book. It involves making any major changes you wish to make, perhaps deleting material, adding material, moving paragraphs around and/or reorganizing.

It also involves dividing your story into chapters. Chapter divisions make a book easier to read, and they make it easier for readers to go back and find specific references. Chapter titles also make each part of your book more enticing.

Many writers simply use the activity titles from *Writing Your Life* as their chapter titles. Others name chapters to fit a major theme that runs through their life, like travel, religion or love of literature. Others base chapter titles upon a lifelong interest or hobby. One woman, for example, gave her chapters the names of quilt patterns. Another used the names of birds. One man used the names of old hymns for his chapter titles, and another simply used spans of years, like 1909 - 1919, or 1920 - 1930.

Another idea is to look at your answer to question #8, from "Who Are You — Really?": *If you could choose a symbol for your life, what would it be?* You might organize your book around that symbol. For example, you might decide your life has been a song and then give each chapter a different song title.

The possibilities are endless. Use your imagination and have some fun planning the organization and/or theme of your book. In doing so, a title for your entire work will probably emerge. For example, you might decide to use "moving" as the theme for your book, because of all the many places you have lived. You could then use different addresses as chapter titles and call the entire book *On the Road Again*.

Choose your title carefully. It is an important first step in grabbing the interest of your readers.

Proofreading

Proofreading is the final step before your book is typed. You need to go over your book and make any corrections necessary in spelling, punctuation, capitalization, sentence structure, etc. After you have gone over it yourself, have someone else go over it again — or even pay a professional proofreader to do it.

It is important to do your best, but don't worry about creating a masterpiece of writing. Your children and grandchildren are sure to love your book, flaws and all.

Beginnings and Endings

Before you are finished with your memoirs, you have just a bit more writing to do — the pages for the beginning of the book and the pages for the end. At a glance, these are the pages you will need:

Beginning:

1. Title page
2. Copyright notice
3. Dedication
4. Acknowledgments
5. Table of Contents
5. Prologue

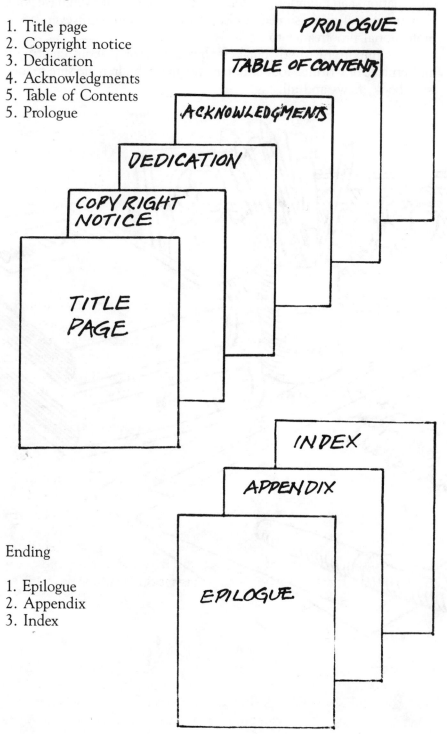

Ending

1. Epilogue
2. Appendix
3. Index

Read on for more information about the beginning and ending pages.

Beginnings

Title Page

On the title page of your book, put the following:

- the title of your book
- your name
- the date the book was completed

Copyright Notice

Include a copyright notice, if desired, on the back of the title page or on a separate page. The copyright notice should include the following:

- the word "copyright." Most notices also include the copyright symbol: © or (c).
- the year the work was completed
- your name

Example: Copyright © 1992 by Mary Borg

Copyright is a form of protection for writers. It gives you the exclusive right to print, reprint, sell and distribute your work. According to current copyright laws, your work is copyrighted as soon as you write it. You probably don't need to take the next step of registering your copyright, unless you want added protection — perhaps because you are printing hundreds of copies of your book, or because you are very well-known.

To register your copyright, write to the Register of Copyrights, Library of Congress, Washington, D.C. 20559. Ask for Circulars R1 and R99 and for Form TX.

Fill out the Form TX carefully. Then include Form TX, three copies of the book (with the notice of copyright included on each) and the $20.00 registration fee, all in the same envelope. (Note: your books will not be returned.)

When the material has been registered, you will receive a certificate verifying the registration of your copyright. Don't be impatient. It may take several months to receive the registration certificate.

Dedication.

The next page should be the dedication page. To whom would you like to dedicate your book? Perhaps you would like to dedicate it to an individual, to your ancestors or to your descendants. The dedication page should include a statement of dedication, often something as simple as, "For my children."

Acknowledgments

If you like, write a statement acknowledging anyone who gave you particular help in preparing your book — perhaps a family member or friend who helped you gather information, locate pictures or type your manuscript. Perhaps you will even want to thank the wife, son or granddaughter who "nagged" you into writing the book in the first place!

Table of Contents

For the table of contents, list the chapter titles and the pages on which they begin. Then be sure to remember to number the pages of your book.

Prologue

As you put together the story of your life, consider writing a prologue. The prologue creates a first impression. It sets the tone for the rest of your book. It is generally easy to write, for you have already completed the hard part — the book itself.

There are no rules for writing a prologue. Make yours as short or as long as you like, as simple or as complex. Only you know what introductory remarks you would like for the opening of your book.

"Begin at the beginning," the King said, gravely, *"and go on till you come to the end; then stop."*

Lewis Carroll, *Alice in Wonderland*

From the prologues of *Writing Your Life* autobiographies:

This is the story of my life, as I remember it. Two people will look at the same rose and have different reactions. One will smell the fragrance and notice the soft folds of the petals. Another might just see the color of the rose and notice the thorns.

So it is with life. We believe what we want to believe. We see what we want to see. We hear what we want to hear.

Living life is not easy. It is taking the lemons we are given and making lemonade that make us flourish and become more perceptive.

Read what you want. Discard what you want. I will still remain one of your ancestors.

Julia L. "Judy" Graham, *My Life*

On January 28, 1988, I will have reached my 77th birthday. I still can't believe I have reached that age.

As people grow older, they have a tendency to relive the past. Some say, "It is over. Never look back." But at my age, I feel that recalling memories is part of living. The nice thing about it is, you don't have to stay at any certain age. You can stray at will through all the levels of time. The most pleasant journeys we take in life are back through memory.

So, as the years unfold, take my hand and let's walk through my childhood, my growing-up years, down the steps into a threshold of history.

Marie Giesler, *Sentimental Journey*

Where I reside at the present time, to avoid trespass, my steps must cease at the lot line, but my heart reaches beyond to the distant bluffs and rolling hills of my birth and early manhood . . . .

To a place where the prairie trails seem to end just over the next rise but really lead to everywhere.

To a place where the Lord still has room, after a summer shower, to form a rainbow in the sky and one of equal hues on the prairie grass, the two bows clasping hands at the horizon to form a circular splendor that few have witnessed.

To a place where the work was hard and the hours long because of necessity, where you pillowed your head in contentment, not exhaustion, a place where each new day was a challenge because each one there had a task to fulfill.

To a place where families and neighbors lived for each other in good times and bad, and shared in each other's joys and sorrows.

To a place where anywhere else was a long way off and the big wide world was scary.

Yet from this era and these prairies and one-room schools came forth doctors, lawyers, merchants and chiefs to meet the challenge of this big wide world. It is of this era and these prairies that I write, to bring forth things that will otherwise be forgotten.

Charles A. Phillips, *Dryland Diary*

Epilogue

The epilogue is your opportunity to add a final touch to your story. Like the prologue, it can be as simple or as detailed as you like.

The epilogue might take the form of a blessing to your descendants. It might be a challenge. It might be a prediction. It might even be a promise for a second volume of your work!

Appendix

An appendix is for any information of interest that doesn't fit anywhere else in your book. It can have several parts, covering a variety of topics.

The appendix might include favorite family recipes or the ingredients for home remedies that your family has found successful over the years. It might include useful bits of family information, like the location of burial plots, the instructions for turning on the water at the mountain cabin, a list of who has what family heirlooms, and the names of the banks in which deeds, wills and other assets are located.

The appendix might include copies of *Writing Your Life* activities that you haven't included elsewhere. Examples might be "Family Tree," "Time Line," "Floor Plan" and "Life's Highs and Lows."

The appendix might also include copies of documents that provide historical authenticity to your story. Those documents could be marriage licenses, church confirmation certificates, naturalization or citizenship papers, death certificates, property deeds or old bills of sale.

The appendix might even include answers to questions that are difficult for you to discuss with family members. Some of those questions might be:

- If you become very ill, what are your medical desires?
- Have you made a living will? If so, where is it?
- Do you wish to be a transplant donor?
- How do you feel about extraordinary life support techniques?
- Are there specific instructions you would like followed for your burial and funeral or memorial service? Are there special songs, Biblical passages, favorite hymns or prayers you would like to have included? Are there certain individuals you would like to participate in the service?
- Where would you like your final resting place to be?

Index

An index is an alphabetical listing of topics and/or names that are mentioned in your book, with the page numbers where they are mentioned. Because compiling an index can be time-consuming, include one only if you feel it is important to your book.

Example:
travels, 22, 95, 99-102
Uncle Joe, 10, 12, 72

"That's all there is, there ain't any more."

Ethel Barrymore

From the epilogues of *Writing Your Life* autobiographies:

I would urge you, at the earliest age possible and using your own system, to accumulate and save details of historical events, great inventions, joys, sorrows, trips, etc. as they happen in your life. Then, in your senior years, write something similar to this book for your family. It is a wonderful experience, as well as a family history. Just don't wait, as I did, until you are seventy-seven years of age to try and remember back that many years.

Pearl Bodendorfer, *Grandmother's Legacy*

I began this chronicle on February 7th, 1985 (my seventy-first birthday), and am now writing this in December, 1985. I have edited and rewritten reams as further memories and observations impinged upon and amplified former, already-written words. . . .

Blushing modesty would normally have prevented me from writing at such great length about so many events in my life, were it not for the sake of family history. Some parts are no doubt trivial, and some more vital to proper perspective. I have no editor with a monstrous blue pencil to eliminate the chaff from the wheat. You can be my editor by skimming over the trivial.

Leading busy lives as you do, I can hardly expect you to reply in kind by writing about your childhoods as you remember our part in them, but it would be very interesting to both Mom and me, some day, to have your viewpoint of those crowded days.

Mark Yurman, *My Biography*

The years from the day we were married until now slipped by very fast. It seems unreal, almost as though I went to bed one night while the children were all small, and woke up to find them grown and gone.

As I write this, I have many fond memories and would not trade them for anything. How proud I am to have such a nice family. You children would make any father proud. You have all been so kind and thoughtful to us. My best wishes that you will have families of your own and that they in turn will return this same love and affection.

I have always said that you children made me toe the mark, and I had to work very hard living up to your expectations. You made me be a better person, knowing that you, all five of you, were there to judge. Yes, I had a father image to play and you made me very much aware of it.

There is a saying in the ranch country that goes something like this: "You can't expect the calf to be any better than the bull." You proved that theory wrong.

Tom Schelly, *Stories of My Life*

Getting Your Book Made

At last you are ready to put your material into book form. Getting a book made can be broken into five main steps:

1. Reproducing photographs
2. Typing
3. Choosing a cover
4. Making copies
5. Binding the book.

1. Reproducing photographs

First, you will need to decide how to reproduce the photographs you want to include in your book. Whatever method you use, remember this: Be sure to include captions for all photographs. Each caption should identify all the people in the picture, as well as the place and approximate date the picture was taken. Also, note each person's relationship to you — maternal great-grandmother, second cousin, daughter, etc. What is obvious to you may not be obvious to future generations.

Photocopying. The easiest and most inexpensive method of reproduction is photocopying. Many photos reproduce reasonably well on a conventional photocopier. It pays to experiment with different settings on the copier, and with different copiers. (Some copiers make much clearer copies than others.)

Many larger cities across the country have photocopying centers like Kinko's, where you can make photocopies for only a few cents per page. Some even have color photocopiers, which will reproduce colored materials reasonably well — but at a much higher price. If you live in a smaller town, you can find photocopiers at many businesses, schools, libraries and even supermarkets.

Halftones. If you are going to have your book printed professionally, rather than photocopied, you will need to have halftones made of your photographs. The printer you select can handle this process.

Reprints. Another option is to have reprints made of your photographs, so that you can attach actual photographs inside each finished book. (Of course, this can be expensive if you are making many copies of your book.) If you don't have the negatives of some photographs, find a store that will make prints from the photographs themselves.

2. Typing

Getting your book into "print" is the next step. That means typing the book. You may want to type it yourself, hire someone to type it or enlist the help of one of your children or grandchildren.

Here are a few basics to keep in mind:

- Clean your typewriter keys and use a new typewriter ribbon.
- Be sure to leave an adequate left-hand margin, taking into account binding space. For most purposes, you will need a lefthand margin of about one and a half inches.
- Number your pages.

Planning ahead. If you want to include photographs, drawings or documents on a page that also includes typing, you will need to do some planning. Here is an easy method to follow:

- Place the photograph, drawing or document where you would like it to be on the finished page.
- Make several photocopies.
- Type directly onto one of the photocopies, creating an illustrated page. (The extra photocopies are for insurance, in case you need to start over.)

Using a computer. If you type your material yourself, now may be the time to learn to use a computer. Computer word processing programs make typing and editing a breeze. It is easy to learn the basics, and you will be amazed by how much you can do on the computer. Instantly, you can correct errors. You can move sentences or paragraphs around. You can delete sentences or paragraphs with just a few strokes of the key. Best of all, you don't have to retype a whole page whenever you decide to change something. All you have to do is make your changes; then the page automatically readjusts itself.

When planning your book, it is a good idea to include photographs, drawings, documents, etc. throughout the text — rather than saving them all until the end. Your finished book will then look more inviting, and it will be more interesting to read.

Typesetting. If you really want to create a professional look, consider having your book typeset. It will be expensive, but you may prefer to spend more money for better results. With typesetting, the print in your book will resemble the higher-quality print you see in books and magazines, instead of the print you see on typewritten documents.

With typesetting, you can choose from many type styles. You also have the flexibility of different sizes of type — larger for headings, smaller for the text, italics for emphasis, etc.

To get your book typeset, take your book to a typesetter and get an estimate. You can find typesetters in the yellow pages of the telephone book, or any printer can recommend one. If you have used a computer, you may be able to cut typesetting costs considerably. Some typesetters can transfer the words from your computer disc onto their machines, thus eliminating the need for retyping. That can save hours — and dollars. Or you can print your document with a laser printer, which produces copy that resembles typesetting, but at a fraction of the cost. (Many offices now use laser printers, and more and more individuals also have them in their homes.)

3. Choosing a cover

For the cover of your book you have many options. You might choose something simple, perhaps plain, colored card stock available at a photocopying center or from a printer. You might want to create an original design, photocopying the design onto card stock. You might want to create a special, personalized cover for each child and grandchild, using your talents for quilting, embroidery, watercolor or calligraphy. Your choices are limited only by your imagination.

Whatever your choice, try to make the cover something that will last, and something that looks inviting.

At a photocopying center, you may be able to combine choosing a cover, making copies and binding your book into one step. The attendant can show you what kinds of card stock, paper and plastic binding are available. You can then have your cover design photocopied onto the card stock, your book photocopied onto your choice of paper, and the cover and copies bound together with plastic binding. Often, copies of your book will be finished in only a few minutes.

4. Making copies

After your book is typed, decide how many copies of the book you want to have made. Make a list of all the people who should receive a copy. Remember to count each child, each grandchild, each of your siblings, special people in your life and perhaps your local library.

Whether you photocopy your book or have it printed, be sure to ask about the availability of acid-free paper, which will preserve your material for a much longer period of time than ordinary paper. You may need to special order the paper, but the added quality will be worth the extra effort and expense.

Photocopying. The easiest and most inexpensive method of reproduction for your book is photocopying. You can photocopy the pages yourself, or you can have a photocopying center do it for you.

If you use a photocopying center, just mention that you want the material collated. Then you won't have to spend time putting the pages in the proper order. Many photocopying machines at such centers will collate the pages automatically.

Printing. If you want a higher-quality reproduction, or if you want to print a large number of copies, consider taking your book to a printer. The overall cost may be high, but the book will have sharper, longer-lasting print. If you order enough copies (at least 200), the cost will probably be less per page than for photocopying. The printer will be able to guide you through the steps necessary in completing a printed book.

Be sure to get an estimate for the job before you get your book printed. It is also wise to shop around and to compare prices.

5. Binding the book

After the pages and/or covers are finished, you will need to bind your book. The easiest binding, for most purposes, is plastic spiral binding, available at photocopy centers and offset printers for only a few dollars (or less) per book. Simply take in the copies of your books, with the covers, and ask the attendant about plastic spiral binding. The books can often be bound while you wait.

Other options for binding include making handbound books, using three-ring notebooks or going to a professional bindery. Professional binding is, of course, much more expensive than other methods. You will need to do some research to find out what is available in your area, and at what cost.

Keep on Writing

Congratulations. You have worked hard to finish your autobiography, and you should feel proud of your accomplishment. You have given your family — and yourself — a special, wonderful gift.

Don't stop now. You have become a writer; keep on writing. Discipline yourself to write in a journal on a daily, weekly or monthly basis. Write about the events of your present day life and about your thoughts and feelings. Or write a second volume of your memoirs, adding more stories from the past or continuing with stories of your life today. Another idea is to experiment, perhaps trying your hand at fiction or poetry.

You might even consider trying to get parts of your work published. Local newspapers and organizations are often interested in publishing stories of the past by local authors. Some national magazines also print such material. Check out the possibilities on a local, state or national level by visiting your local library reference section. One useful guide you will find there is *Writer's Market* (published yearly by F&W Publications). It is full of information about preparing a manuscript and submitting it for publication. It includes the names and addresses of book publishers, consumer publications, and trade, technical and professional journals.

Whatever you do, don't give up. The more you write, the more you will think of to write about. *Writing* your life can become a *way* of life.

Enjoy it.

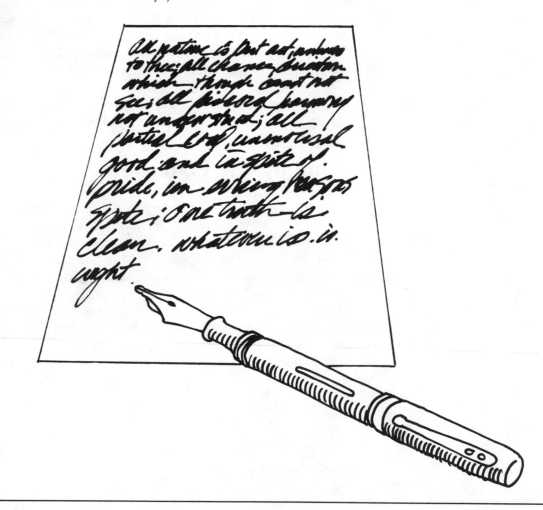

Cottonwood Press Materials for Adults . . . .

Writing Your Life, by Mary Borg, is available from Cottonwood Press for **$15.95**. You may also be interested in other Cottonwood Press materials for adults, listed below:

Writing Your Life Teacher Edition, by Mary Borg. The *Teacher Edition* is a comprehensive guide that includes detailed, flexible lesson plans for a *Writing Your Life* class, ideas for adapting the class to fit a variety of shorter formats, suggested readings for class, ideas for what to do when a class needs "jazzing up," and teacher tips for helping seniors succeed at writing. (To be used with basic *Writing Your Life* text, above) **$21.95**

Exercise SeniorStyle, by Susan Malmstadt and Marilynn Freier. *Exercise SeniorStyle* is a set of two different, 30-minute videos in one package, designed by experienced instructors just for senior adults. With *Exercise SeniorStyle*, seniors get a real workout — but one that is designed for their safety and success. The tapes feature both seated and standing exercises, done to original, upbeat music. **$34.95**

Exercise SeniorStyle Guide for Instructors, by Susan Malmstadt and Marilynn Freier. With the *Exercise SeniorStyle Guide for Instructors* , nearly any interested, committed individual can learn to teach an effective exercise class for senior adults. The book gives basic, practical information in an easy-to-read fashion — everything from choosing appropriate music and encouraging reluctant male exercisers to learning safety precautions and adapting exercises to fit the level of different exercise groups. (To be used with the *Exercise SeniorStyle* videotapes, above) **$9.95**

Quantity	Name of Item	Price Each	TOTAL PRICE

Name _____

Address _____

City_____ State_____ Zip_____

Payment:

☐ Check   ☐ VISA   ☐ MasterCard   ☐ Purchase Order

VISA/MasterCard
Number _____

Expiration Date _____

Signature _____

Make Checks Payable to:
COTTONWOOD PRESS, INC.
305 W. Magnolia, Suite 398
Fort Collins, CO 80521
(303) 493-1286
970

COTTONWOOD PRESS

Shipping & Handling

	Add		Add
$10.00 & under	$1.00	$45.01-$75.00	$5.50
$10.01-$25.00	$2.25	$75.01-$100.00	$6.50
$25.01-$35.00	$3.50	Over $100.00	$8.00
$35.01-$45.00	$4.50		

Amount Ordered	
Colorado residents add 3% sales tax	
Shipping and handling (see chart)	
TOTAL	